What others are saying about this book:

"This book is for the person who doesn't know anything about getting anything printed." - Magazine Design and Production.

"The author concentrates on various techniques that are at once inexpensive and fast to allow the book to get into print quickly and at little cost. Recommended." - The Reference Book Review.

"Here are the technical details on how to get your poetry published at your local quick print shop." - Writer's Digest magazine.

"If you're planning to produce between a few hundred copies and a couple of thousand copies of your book, get hold of this knowledgeable guide right away. It covers everything from composition and layout to covers and binding." - How to Get Happily Published by Judith Appelbaum and Nancy Evans.

"...simple and direct with many clear illustrations. It makes you want to publish a book right away!" - Travel Writer's Market Letter.

"Introduces modern techniques and machinery that make it possible to turn company reports and sales presentations into bound books quickly and inexpensively." - The Office magazine

"This is an ideal do-it-yourself system." - Quick Printing magazine.

"It is extremely thorough, full of new ideas and the very latest techniques, and is very nicely illustrated." - The Armiger's News.

This book will save you a lot of money

Publishing Short-Run Books
How To Paste up and Reproduce Books
Instantly Using Your Quick Print Shop

by Dan Poynter

Fifth Revised Edition

Para Publishing, Santa Barbara, California

Publishing Short-Run Books

How To Paste Up and Reproduce Books Instantly Using Your Quick Print Shop

by Dan Poynter

Published by

Para Publishing
Post Office Box 4232
Santa Barbara, CA 93140-4232, USA

Library of Congress Cataloging In Publication Data
     Poynter, Daniel F.
     Publishing Short-Run Books.
     How To Paste up and Reproduce Books
     Instantly Using Your Quick Print Shop.
     Bibliography: p. Includes index.
     1. Self publishing. I. Title.
     Z285.5.P68 070.5'068 80-13614
     ISBN 0-915516-61-6

Table of Contents

About The Author

Dan Poynter fell into publishing. He spent eight years researching a labor of love and after discussing the publishing industry with other authors, he decided to self-publish. The technical book on parachutes sold and his new career was launched.

In 1973, Dan became interested in a new aviation sport. Unable to find a book on the subject, he sat down and wrote one. *Hang Gliding* has been through the press ten times for 130,000 in print so far: a *best seller*.

Continuing to write, he has produced 27 books, some of which have been translated into Spanish, Japanese, Russian, British English, Italian and German. Although he initially concentrated on aviation sports, Dan has become one of the most successful general author/publishers.

Dan has been setting type with computers since 1980. He pioneered strike-on typesetting with impact printers and developed many of the typesetting and binding techniques mentioned in this book.

Dan has become a widely acknowledged proponent of small press publishing and is the creator of numerous innovative book marketing techniques. He conducts book promotion seminars in his home/office in Santa Barbara, California.

In his brief publishing career, Dan has sold over a half-million books for more than two million dollars. Many of his books sell at the rate of a steady 10,000 copies per year, every year.

Dan was prompted to write this book by the many writers who wish to get into print inexpensively. He shows how to make a quick, small print run, shortcutting all the usual start-up costs. Here is the fast, easy and inexpensive way to break into print with your own book.

Acknowledgement

Many people helped to make this book possible. Some were an inspiration and some provided valuable information while others supplied needed editorial talent.

I am deeply indebted to Mindy Bingham of Advocacy Press, Linda Allen DeBlanco of Forget-Me-Not Publishing, Paul Orfalea of Kinko's Graphics Corporation, Jan Venolia, author of *Write Right!*, Rory Donaldson of Endurance, Bill Friday, author of *Instant Printing 2*, Milt Strong of Technical Documentation Service, Walter B. Graham, graphic arts consultant with Idea Seminars, publisher Robbie Fanning, John Fergusson our advisor and Mary Mansfield and Tom Cole of Kinko's Graphics by Cole. Then, of course, I must acknowledge the help and support I received from my able assistant Monique Tihanyi.

I sincerely thank all these fine people. I know they are proud of the parts they have played in the development of the new approaches to book production described in this manual as well as their contribution to the production of this book.

Several trade names are mentioned in this book. They have been capitalized.

Cover by Robert Howard

Chapter One

Into Print—Quickly And Inexpensively

The prestige enjoyed by the published author is unparalleled in our society. Publishing a book establishes the writer as an expert in his or her field, a position which often leads to job advancement, high-paying consulting work and even a new career. People have always held books in high regard. Authors are opinion molders—a major force in our communities.

Many people self-publish because they are dealing with subject matter that is too limited to interest a large commercial publisher (or the large New York publishers do not have the imagination to recognize the potential of the book.) Other authors reason that they want to get to market sooner, maintain

control of their work or make more money from
their efforts.

In self-publishing the author takes the responsi-
bility for the entire production as well as the
marketing of the book. A "publisher" is defined as
the one who puts up the money. He or she is the
"producer"; the one who sees that all the ingredients
of the book get put together, including graphics,
paper, printing, binding, getting to market, and
publicizing the book's availability. He or she may
receive financial help from family or friends and
some parts of the production or marketing may be
farmed out. Self-publishing occurs everywhere and
consists of everything from grammar school class
newsletters to large, fine books.

Self-Publishing is not *vanity* or *subsidy* publishing
where a company charges the author to publish the
book. Many vanity publishing firms have established a poor track record over the years. If they
delivered all the marketing and distribution work
their contracts *seem* to promise, the alternative they
offer might be a good one. However, too often they
only bind a few books (knowing they will not need
more because the book will not sell), do little if any
promotion and charge a very high price. Anyone considering this route to publishing should compare a
vanity publisher's quotes with those of regular book
printers.

**See the Glossary in the Appendix of this book for defini-
tions of words that are new to you**

Do-it-yourself book publishing, or self-publishing, is becoming increasingly popular (in fact, in California there are far more author-publishers than there are regular publishers). Many authors and educators are turning to neighborhood quick print shops for the production of their short-run books; they bypass the middlemen and handle their own marketing and distribution. They invest their time as well as their money, but the rewards are far greater. They get it all, not having to share the pie with a whole establishment of helpers.

Self-publishing is not new. In fact, it has solid early American roots; it is almost a tradition. Many authors have elected to go their own way after being turned down by regular publishers, while many others have decided to do it themselves from the beginning. Well-known self-publishers include Mark Twain, Zane Grey, Upton Sinclair, Carl Sandburg, James Joyce, D.H. Lawrence, Ezra Pound, Edgar Rice Burroughs, Stephen Crane, Mary Baker Eddy, George Bernard Shaw, Edgar Allen Poe, Rudyard Kipling, Henry David Thoreau, Walt Whitman, Richard Nixon and many, many more. Do-it-yourself publishing is accepted.

Many self-publishers find that once they have proven their books in the marketplace, they are approached by big publishing houses with offers to print a new edition. It is far easier to interest a publisher in a book with a track record than in an untried manuscript. Some authors use self-publishing to break into the big time while others prefer to publish their own material, retaining the work, control and extra money for themselves.

Self-publishing is the ideal system for educators needing just a few copies for a class, poets who desire a small private printing, publishers who wish to test the market before investing in a large print run, corporate sales presentations, printers who want to make a dummy book to check the design and make a final proofreading, and just anyone who is in a hurry to break into print.

The self-publishing educator. To most educators, being published by a major firm is a dream. To those working under a publish or perish threat, the dream may be a nightmare. Yet most instructors will never see their years of work in book form. Short-run, self-publishing offers the educator the opportunity to get into print inexpensively in order to prove and improve the material in school use. Custom-made books provide the teacher with maximum control over content; any combination of text, journal articles and other materials may be included. Since only a few books are manufactured, it is easy and inexpensive to update the information by adding or deleting material.

Educators have some interesting marketing choices for their books. They may sell them directly to their students, have their department, school or agency purchase them for resale or have the bookstore buy them in quantity for distribution.

Some copy shops established near universities use short-run printing techniques to provide students with customized course materials. Professors leave their notes, articles and study aids at the shop and the shop photocopies one copy at a time, on demand.

New techniques produce books faster and for less. Book production used to be a very expensive proposition. Thousands of copies had to be printed to justify the investment in typesetting and platemaking setup costs. Today, the printing industry is caught up in a revolution. New equipment and techniques are completely changing book production. Personal computers with laser printers allow the author to write the book and to set the type. Instant print shops are turning out excellent work on new machinery which bypasses many of the intermediate pre-press steps used by regular commercial printers. Now, many of these quick print shops are doing their very short-run reproduction on xerographic machines instead of offset presses. Some photocopy machines require hardly any setup time, can be operated by less-expensive personnel, print both sides of the pages, sort them, and provide more consistent work. Other copy machines do a nice job on photographs and some will even reproduce color. Xerographic machines are currently turning out 100 billion pages each year.

The big news, though, and the missing links in the book production chain are typesetting and binding. Until recently, those wishing to take advantage of low-priced copy shop work were limited in what they could submit to be copied. One could use a typewriter or spend a lot more money to have the manuscript typeset by a graphic arts shop. Now the personal computer with laser printer is changing all that. The word processor provides professional-looking copy at in-house prices, and the information is stored on a disk for easy, inexpensive updating.

Another recently developed technique makes it possible to install "perfect binding" type soft covers that look as though they were part of a multi-thousand binding machine run. Now with the word processor, laser typesetting, xerography, and this new binding process, an author may shortcut the book production system and get into print far faster, for a smaller up-front investment.

The cost. Today, three basic types of printing are of interest to book manufacturers:

1. Xerography is ideally suited to press runs under 200 copies. It is very fast and the pages are collated automatically. Photo reproduction using these *plain paper* copiers is fair to good depending upon the copy machine used. Xerographic services are normally found in copy shops.

Xerography is the least expensive in the very short run. This is because there is little set up time, no plate making and the pasteup is done by the customer. Many copy shops will photocopy both sides of a sheet of paper (yielding four pages in a 5.5 x 8.5 book) for five or six cents each in quantity. Covers may be installed professionally or you may do the work yourself following the instructions in this book. Best of all, the books look just like the expensively produced tomes in the book stores.

2. Instant printing with a direct image system is economical between 200 and 2500 copies. The

automated shops use paper plates and specialized small offset presses. Photograph reproduction is good. Instant printing is found in quick print shops.

3. Quality offset lithography, using more expensive negatives and metal plates, is offered by regular commercial print shops and some fast printers. Metal plates are good for longer press runs and, ultimately, a lower per-unit cost. They should be used where the highest quality photographs are required. Offset printing offers a greater choice of inks and paper and it is economical over two or three thousand impressions. To get an idea of prices, send for a Publisher's Planning Kit to Delta Lithograph Co., 28210-P North Avenue Stanford, Valencia, CA 91355.

Copyright

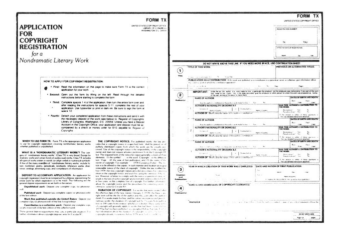

The Copyright Form

Copyright is a statutory right obtained by writers and others to prevent reproduction of their work without their consent. Basically, anything you write belongs to you. For $10, the Government will register your book and keep a copy on file. Copyrights work both ways: they protect your work from others and their work from you. Since January 1, 1978, the copyright term has been extended for the author's life plus fifty years. It is now a valuable part of your estate, so be certain your copyrighted material is mentioned in your will.

For more free information on copyright, write to the Copyright Office, Library of Congress, Washington, DC 20559. Ask for circular R99 and a couple of copies of Form TX.

Handmade books? Originally, books were made by hand. People not only wrote the words, they made the paper, set the type and handcrafted the covers. Today we have machines that produce books faster, more efficiently and with greater consistency in quality. These machines have allowed us to produce more books, spreading the costs to realize a lower per-unit price. The problem is that the printing and binding machines must be set up for each production run and preparing the machines for production takes time. In fact, for a very short run, the setup time may cost more than the running time. Those wishing just a few copies of a book may find the per-unit cost to be unacceptable.

For those who wish to produce a very short run of quality books, handmade techniques are still available. And now there are some new smaller, inexpensive machines that make short-run book production economical. You may purchase the machines or visit a print shop that offers the service.

Demand printing. "Demand printing" is the production of only enough copies of a document when and where there is a market for them. It combines handmade single-copy production with new tools to fit new needs. With demand printers at several widely dispersed locations, information can be sent over telephone lines to print books or reports at their destination in order to save time and shipping costs. New technology is making short run publishing, even just a single copy of a lengthy document or book, less expensive than regular printing. This technology permits creation of typeset-appearing printed originals at photocopy machine speed directly from electronically stored text. Eliminated are large print runs and investments in inventory.

An example would be the storage of this book in disk form at your nearby photocopy shop. The book is committed to paper only when a customer requests it. An added advantage is that corrections and updates can be made to the disks periodically and mailed (or sent over telephone lines) to the copy shop. The book being sold is always up-to-date.

Here is an example of a variation on this idea. Para Publishing provides several books on various aspects of book publishing. One popular product consists of nearly twenty different types of publishing contracts. The product is supplied on computer disk so that the buying publisher does not have to retype the contract into his or her machine prior to customizing it. So, Para Publishing sends only the report cover, a cover sheet with directions and a computer disk. The first thing the recipient does is to insert the disk into his or her computer and print out a copy of the book, three hole punch it and insert it into the report folder. This exercise has an added advantage: it demonstrates to the purchaser how easy it is to print out the contracts. Para Publishing reproduces a few disks at a time and does not have to print, store or ship an inventory of several thousand hard copies.

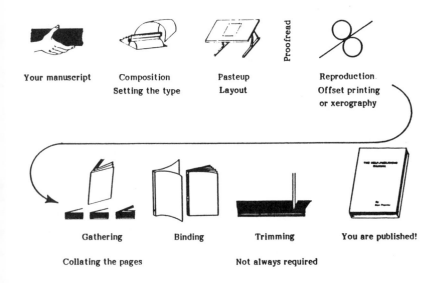

Your manuscript	Composition Setting the type	Pasteup Layout	Proofread	Reproduction. Offset printing or xerography

Gathering Collating the pages	Binding	Trimming Not always required	You are published!

Flow chart

Chapter Two

Format—How Your Book Will Look

This explanation of the book production process is meant to be brief and yet provide enough information to deal with the local printer. For more information, there are many good, detailed books on the art of printing; see the resource section in the Appendix.

Most local quick print shops have the capability to produce your book using either of the modern reproduction methods: offset lithography or xerography.

For print runs in black ink and under 200 copies, your printer will normally choose xerography. This is relatively inexpensive as it avoids setup (plate making) charges. Many people prefer xerography for its denser black type which increases legibility. Avoiding plates also means less production time.

Book size. Most quick print shops use the smaller, less expensive presses and copiers that accept letter size (8.5 x 11) and legal size (8.5 x 14) paper. Therefore, the most economical book sizes are 8.5 x 11 and 5.5 x 8.5 (8.5 x 11 folded once). Thicker legal size stock may be used for wrap-around covers. Any variation from these standards will increase wastage, require more sophisticated equipment and decrease efficiency. End result: higher cost.

Since 5.5 x 8.5 is a standard book size, it fits the shelf well. Another standard, 8.5 x 11, should only be used when there are maps, drawings, charts or other illustrations requiring a larger format. A drawback of the larger size is that the books cannot be saddle stitched (spine stapled) unless printed on an 11 x 17 offset press which is more expensive than xerography (more on this below under "binding"). Furthermore, the book will not be as thick in the 8.5 x 11 format and will not have the same feel of quality. A 120-page book of 5.5 x 8.5 pages is much nicer than a 60-page book of 8.5 x 11 pages. Check with your print shop before deciding on a size.

Eight pages are required to qualify for the Postal Service "Book Rate," 50 for a Library of Congress Catalog Card Number and 100 to qualify for a listing in H.W. Wilson's Cumulative Book Index. Over 100 pages is psychologically good and will help to justify your price. So, if you have just 99 pages, add some copy or an illustration.

Keep the book short. The reader who values his or her time may be intimidated by a thick tome. If you are selling fiction (entertainment), a thick book provides more for the money. But in nonfiction (valuable information), it is best to deliver the goods as briefly and concisely as possible. Give quality, not quantity.

Paper. Paper is available in a variety of weights, sizes, textures, colors and qualities, but you will probably be dealing with *bond* paper or *book* paper and cover stock. Twenty lb. bond is the common copy shop paper while 50 lb. and 60 lb. book are common in texts. Actually, 20 lb. *bond* and 50 lb. *book* are the same. Heavier book papers cost more but lend the feeling of quality. Heavy, glossy cover stock is easily handled by both offset presses and most xerographic machines. For xerography, the stock must be smooth; no textured paper. Again, ask your printer what he normally stocks; standardize and save money. Paper is covered in detail in Chapter Five.

Dividers of colored paper are sometimes used in certain academic applications. They cannot be installed in a saddle stitched book because they would wrap around and appear twice as often as necessary and half would be in the wrong place. However, they are easy to install in perfect-bound 5.5 x 8.5 and 8.5 x 11 books. Dividers may be printed or plain and may be on regular or heavy stock.

Ink. The text of books are printed in black ink because there is rarely a good reason to use another color. Xerographic machines that will reproduce color exist but they are expensive to operate. There-fore, you will probably choose to have color work done with offset presses; they require an extra setup charge as the press has to be cleaned out and refitted with the colored ink.

Binding. The binding is the packaging for your book—the final touch. Although there are many ways to cover a book, the choice will be made on the basis of the market (who will buy it) and expected usage (will it be read once or used repeatedly as a manual?)

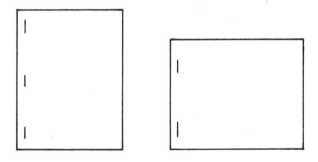

Side stitched: Sturdy but will not lie flat when opened.

A variety of binding styles are available through quick print shops. Some types can be bound in-house while others must be subcontracted out.

1. **"Wire stitches"** are staples and may be used in binding softcover books. They come from a roll of wire and are adjustable in length. This is the least expensive binding method and may be done with hand operated tools or highly automated machinery.

Holland tape: Improved appearance.

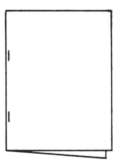

Saddle Stitched: Attractive, lies flat when opened but limited to about eighty pages (twenty sheets).

Wire stitches may be "saddle stitched" where the staple is on the fold or "side stitched" where the staple is driven through from the front to the back cover. Saddle stitching is limited to about twenty sheets (eighty pages) of paper, depending upon the thickness of the stock because of the amount of paper "lost" in wrapping around the spine. Side stitching will not permit the book to open and lay flat so it should not be used in manuals. Sometimes

"Holland Tape" is used to dress up the book by covering the side stitched staples.

2. **"Perfect" binding** is the standard glued-on cover you see on most softcover books; this book is an example. In perfect binding, the cover is wrapped around and glued to the raw edges of the text. One great advantage is that it presents a squared-off spine on which the title and name of the author may be printed. A text of more than fifty pages is required for a square spine. Perfect binding is more expensive than wire stitching but is more attractive. If you want your product to sell like a book, it will have to look like a book. Until recently it was necessary to set up for a large binding run to install perfect bound covers. Chapter Five describes an inexpensive short-run method.

3. **Cloth binding** (case binding or hard binding) consists of securing the pages with sewing, staples or glue and then installing them between two hard paper boards. Hardcover books will tolerate a lot more abuse and are therefore preferred by libraries. They are comparatively expensive due to the cost of materials and the setup charges, but they are first rate.

4. **Spiral wire** binding will allow the book to open up and lie flat but it has a poor shelf appearance because the title cannot be printed on the spine. Another drawback is that manufacture requires special machinery. Plastic comb binding has replaced spiral wire in many shops.

5. **Plastic comb** binding may be installed on any book up to some 400 sheets and two inches thick. Comb binding allows the book to lie flat and pages may be added or removed. It is more expensive (thirty cents to $4.50 depending upon the length of the spine, the thickness of book and the quantity of books being bound) than perfect binding and makes the product appear more like a manual than a book. Comb-bound books do not stack well, thus making shipping a chore, and they are not acceptable to bookstores since the title cannot be read when the book is displayed spine-out. The irony is that comb binding is expensive while it appears to be cheap. However, comb binding is very popular for short-run academic texts and for industry manuals.

6. **Velo Bind** is similar to side wire stitches but uses melted plastic rivets and a strip of plastic down the edges of the covers. This toughest of all bindings may be used to install soft "document covers" or special Velo Bind hard covers.

7. **Cheshire** has an interesting hot melt hard and soft cover binding machine that is good for short-run production. It is especially useful for reports and catalogs where it is often desirable to remove and replace pages. Employing new techniques, it may be used to produce a perfect bound type cover of your own design. The method is explained in Chapter Five.

8. **Three-ring binders** are sometimes used in very expensive manuals directed towards professionals. They allow the easy addition of updated material,

but they are expensive and the pages tear out easily.

Page numbering. Pages may be numbered sequentially from the first page to the last or from the beginning to the end of each section. Numbering by *section* is useful in books which will be updated regularly; when employing this method, be sure to indicate the section in your numbering scheme (e.g., I-1 or A-1).

Design. The placement of the sections in this book is typical and may be used as a model for your own work. Pay particular attention to the order of the pages as well as the placement and design of the front matter (the pages leading up to Chapter One). The location of the copyright page is important, for example. This brief text shows you **How** to construct a book while *The Self-Publishing Manual* explains **why**. See the Appendix.

Some quick print shops offer design help and charge for it, but many are printers not designers. Do not expect your printer to lay out your book without compensation. Layout is covered in Chapter Four.

Chapter Three

Composition—Words onto Paper

There are numerous ways to record your message: handwritten, typewritten, typeset and so on. Here are some basic considerations and descriptions of the various choices. Modern printing methods will photographically reproduce any dark mark on a light surface, such as black ink on white paper. For more details, see the Resource section in the Appendix. Here are some considerations.

Right-margin justification. This book, newspapers and most magazines have an even right-hand margin which is more professional in appearance than a "ragged right." Ordinarily justification is accomplished by adding spaces between the words of the shorter lines to make them equal in length to the longest line. This can be done with any typewriter by tedious count and typing the page twice, once normally and once expanded. The newer, more expensive typesetting machines justify automatically with a memory playback.

Books should be typeset with a justified right-hand margin while lab manuals and workbooks are acceptable with a ragged right format. In the academic world, the quality of the written material is more important than the quality of the graphics, and price is always a major consideration. Your choice will be made considering the market for your written product, your skills, the equipment available and the value you place on your own time. For example, it may be much less expensive to send your work to a secretarial service with sophisticated word processing equipment than to laboriously typewrite the material yourself. It all depends upon your own situation.

Proportional spacing. Most typewriters allow the same space for each character while most typeset copy adjusts the space to the width of the individual letter or number. For example, a proportionally-spaced "i" would receive less horizontal space than a "W." Here are examples:

Proportional spacing vs. constant pitch spacing.
Proportional Spacing vs. constant pitch spacing.

Consequently, constant pitch type appears to be from a typewriter whereas proportionally spaced copy looks like it has been typeset.

Type size. Typewriters produce work in two basic sizes. Pica or "ten pitch" has ten letters to the running inch while elite or "twelve pitch" produces twelve. "Point size" is a printing term used when referring to type height; there are 72 points to the inch. Some type styles such as the IBM Selectric's

ORATOR TYPEFACE

are 14 and 8 point. Orator appears to be much larger but it is still just ten pitch in width. If you are using a typewriter, have a lot of material, wish to save space and your intended audience is younger with good eyesight, try a twelve pitch typeface.

Some people find the smaller 12 pitch type easier to read because of the increased amount of white space between the lines.

```
IBM COURIER Type finds wide use in genera
dence, offset reproduction and manifoldir
square-serif design in the PICA family.
ABCDEFGHIJKLMNOPQRSTUVWXYZ    !@#$%¢&*()_
abcdefghijklmnopqrstuvwxyz    1234567890-
```

Courier: 10 pitch—8 point

```
IBM COURIER 12 Type is ideal for general correspo
reproduction and a wide variety of general applic.
quire the maximum use of typing space.
ABCDEFGHIJKLMNOPQRSTUVWXYZ      !@#$%¢&*()_+¼:",.?
abcdefghijklmnopqrstuvwxyz      1234567890-=½;',./
```

Courier 12: 12 pitch—8 point

Type may also be reduced (more on this later) but reductions are rather complicated for those who do not use this method regularly so it is not recommended for everyone.

If you can type. If you can type, you may do all the typesetting yourself. If you cannot, there are alternatives but first we will discuss how you may do-it-yourself.

Electric typewriter. In order to obtain clear, clean lettering that will result in bright, crisp printed lines, your electric typewriter must have a carbon ribbon. Manual typewriters do not produce even impressions.

If you do not have access to an electric typewriter, rent one. Check the *Yellow Pages* under "stationers" or "typewriter sales." If you use a rental typewriter only to type your final copy, you will not need it very long and the rental price should be quite reasonable.

There are a number of good, new electric type writers on the market but few are as versatile as the IBM Correcting Selectric III, Remington electric and the Xerox electric (manufactured for Xerox by Remington). They have interchangeable "ball" typefaces, print ten or twelve letters to the inch, have a carbon ribbon and the lift-off correcting ability. This last feature is one of the most important as it assures fast, easy, clean corrections. These machines do not have proportional spacing, automatic right margin justification, or small typefaces like professionally set type. Be careful of other lighter, cheaper machines. They may not make a firm, clear impression.

IBM Executive. The Executive provides professional-looking copy because it produces proportionally spaced type. Proportional spacing looks good but it makes right-handed justification even more tedious. Executives have only one typeface per machine and they seem to need adjustment more often.

The Executive has been replaced by the new and more expensive electronics so while you cannot buy them new, there are Executives on the used typewriter market for $300 to $500. One source is Gersten Business Machines, Inc., 37-P West 43rd Street, New York, NY 10036.

Electronic typewriters. Smart typewriters are becoming the new office standard and are replacing the electrical-mechanical models. Designed from the ground up, they are electronically controlled with very few moving parts. Electronic typewriters automate some functions such as centering, underlining and (if they have a memory) final typing.

Many of these smart typewriters use a daisywheel typing element and are relatively quiet. They have a lift-off correcting capability and remember the last several words typed. With this feature, "erasures" up to a full line are made at the touch of a key.

Most electronic typewriters do not have an external, removable memory system such as a disk and their internal, non-removable memories are not permanent. Except for those machines fitted with batteries, the memory is erased when the power is shut off.

Basically, smart typewriters can be divided into three groups: those that remember and can correct up to a couple of lines; those that store up to 1,000 characters and can print them out; and those with larger memories that can be fully edited. It is hard to tell where smart typewriters stop and word processors begin.

Typing hints. Using the layout specifications in the next chapter, simply type your material exactly as you want it to appear in your book. Your quick print shop will reproduce it using a photographic process.

Clean your keys before typing to assure clean, sharp copy. Experiment with the impression control and try a few lines using a second sheet of paper, a single sheet and a plastic second sheet. The platen roller should be reasonably new, hard and smooth. Make sure the machine is well adjusted and that none of the keys are striking off-center.

BASKERVILLE
You're an in-plant printer and
to you for help. Some come wi
ABCDEFGHIJKLMNOPQR
abcdefghijklmnopqrstuvwxyz
1234567890

Serif

CHELMSFORD
You're an in-plant printer an
to you for help. Some come
ABCDEFGHIJKLMNOPQRST
abcdefghijklmnopqrstuvwxy
1234567890

Sans serif

Use a typewriter with a standard serif typeface (serif type has extra lines projecting from the ends of the letters to make them easier to read.) Make your product look like a book by avoiding script, old English, OCR and other odd styles.

If you are using a word processor with a Diablo-type printer or an electronic typewriter with a daisy wheel to produce strike-on type, use a metal print wheel. The cheaper plastic models lose their shape with repeated use, resulting in inconsistent print quality.

Maintain consistent style throughout the book. Do not vary the chapter heads, subheads, indentations or placement of other regular items.

The best impressions are made with a single-strike carbon ribbon. The multi-strike ribbons produce a grayer copy. Cloth ribbons, cotton or silk, tend to over-ink when new and they produce fuzzy letters. If the type is not clean and sharp, stark black on white, the type in the book will not be crisp.

When using a carbon ribbon, allow the type to dry overnight to avoid smearing it. Some people protect their work with a light fogging of a clear spray but most insert a slip sheet of plain paper and are simply careful not to touch the typed page.

Typewriter corrections. Minor corrections are best made employing the lift-off capability of the correcting typewriters. These machines actually remove the ink from the paper. Corrections of several words or lines are best made by typing up the new material and pasting it over the old with rubber cement. The "white out" type of correction tape should never be used as it will not cover well enough, while touch-up opaquing liquids should be used only to clean up illustrations or to block out a single letter. A good test is to place the corrected page on a table under normal light. If the offending letter shows through, the camera will see it too.

Word processors with letter-quality character printers. Dedicated word processors offer quality work with an editing capability. Designed for office use, they are revolutionizing the manufacture of pamphlets and books. They are not inexpensive and yet they are replacing electric typewriters in many applications. Word processors may be out of reach of most new and struggling authors, but many people have access to them in offices and academic communities. It is even possible to rent time on them at some word processing centers and quick print shops. Writers who do not have access to such a machine may be able to use one through a secretarial service.

Word processors are micro processor (computer) controlled typewriters. They automatically justify the right-hand margin, provide storage of the material on magnetic cards, cassette tapes or disks and most have proportional spacing. Usually the storage is on a floppy disk which looks like a small record in a square plastic jacket. Each one holds between 30 and 500 pages of text depending on the type. Many word processors have a printer which will produce a good strike-on type providing camera-ready copy.

Word processors are a great time saver. They eliminate re-typing and all the proofing of that typing. They are ideal for writers (and executives). Users may type in their thoughts, move the words around until they are satisfied and then just push a button for the final copy. The redundant retyping function is eliminated. Word processors with character printers fill the gap in modern book production, shortcutting the whole composition/layout make-ready process.

Revised portions of a long document may be indicated in the margin so that only the changes need be proofed. The revision marks can be made to show on the screen but not on the printout.

Print wheels may be changed to offer a variety of type styles. Three will normally be more than enough: **"Bold P.S."** (proportional space), "Bold *Italic* P.S." and "Spokesman 10." But even with a single print wheel, several possibilities are offered: Upper/Lower case or all CAPS may be set normally, in **bold** or with underlining.

For those who desire the size versatility of photocomposition type, most word processors may be interfaced with these machines. Some typesetting firms offer these services in major cities.

Computers with laser Printers. For the smaller and newer publisher, these are exciting times. A lot of interesting new software for personal computer typesetting is suddenly available. Capabilities are up, prices are coming down and the possibilities are nearly limitless.

"Desktop publishing" is the new buzzword in computers and like many new terms, it is a misnomer—particularly for book publishers. It should be called "PC typesetting" since the technology simply allows us to set type on our own personal computers, in-house rather than send it out. Everything else we do in publishing is the same: writing, editing and sending the boards out to be shot and printed.

The 300 dpi (dots per inch) laser printers do a fine job of typesetting. Some people say the slightly ragged edges (under magnification) of the characters reminds them of those produced with wet ink and hot type. The only people who seem to dislike laser typesetting are those who stand to lose the most—typesetters.

The state of the industry: Currently, there are three basic levels in computer-based laser typesetting systems.

1. The Apple Macintosh with Pagemaker page layout software and the Apple LaserWriter printer.

The MAC is easy to use, does a great job, especially considering the relatively low price and the technology is here now. Anyone who already has a MAC should buy Pagemaker, MacPaint, MacDraw and all the other Apple desktop publishing software and start setting type. In many localities, it is not necessary to purchase a LaserWriter as printer time can be rented cheaply at many copy shops. In other words, it is possible to buy into the system a piece at a time.

On the other hand, if you want your machine to perform other office functions, there is a greater choice of software with the IBM-type system. Remember the most important basic rule of computer purchasing: decide what you want to do, select your software first and then find a machine to run it.

2. The IBM-XT with a page layout program and a laser printer such as the H-P LaserJet Series II.

The IBM-XT (and workalikes) is the most popular machine—more than 5-million are in use. Much more software and many peripherals are available for it. The challenge is to find the right combination of software and peripherals to achieve the desired results for your particular type of book publishing.

IBM-AT class machines such as the Compaq 286 cost a couple of thousand dollars more but work faster and will hold their resale value longer because they are more recent technology. Computers using the 386 chip are faster still.

The problem with the IBM system is that you must (some say "get to") build your own system. You must organize the hard disk, load the software and know how to move around in DOS.

3. The large black on white screens showing a full 8.5 x 11 page with icons such as the Xerox, Kodak, Intran and Interleaf. Cost: from $9,000 to many tens of thousands of dollars.

Most of these packages will not run MS-DOS software or will not work MS-DOS documents in the page layout mode. Therefore, they are "dedicated page layout machines."

Today we must not only select a popular operating system (with lots of software) now and in the future (such as MS-DOS) and a computer from a stable company (such as IBM—and some of its workalikes), now we must select word processing, page layout and other software which will continue to be popular and therefore continue to be supported. The software must grow, change, evolve and improve. Somehow, we must predict which typesetting software is good now and will be the best and most popular in the future.

There are three types of applicable laser printer typesetting software:

1. Word processing such as Microsoft *Word, Wordstar 2000, WordPerfect* and *Spellbinder.* Word processing software may be used to write and edit your book.

2. Font software such as *Laser Fonts*. Font software may be used with a laser printer to give your book a typeset look.

3. Page layout programs such as *PageMaker and Ventura Publisher*. A good page makeup program has fonts and some word processing built into it. These programs make it easier to layout your pages.

Consider the following when purchasing a system. All specifications may not be available at this time and some are more important than others but the perfect system would have them all.

1. A full page display. The page may be 8.5 x 11 or 5.5 x 8.5. For a 5.5 x 8.5 book, the image area is 4.125 x 7.125 with a centered page number at the bottom, so you really need 4.25 x 7.5. If you are publishing 8.5 x 11 books, the software must work easily in two columns. Whether you are typing correspondence or laying out books or brochures, it is much nicer to see the whole page rather than flipping or scrolling endlessly up and down.

Microsoft-*Word* word processing software with an enhanced graphics board and monitor will allow you to see 43 lines on the screen. This is enough to see all of the type in a 5.5 x 8.5 book except the page number. The color screen is a bonus as it is much cheerier than stark black and green.

2. A black-on-white display. Pages should look like pages. Many people find b/w screens much easier on the eyes than green or amber monitors.

B/w monitors are an available extra and some XT workalikes come with b/w screens. A good alternative to the b/w screen is an enhanced color monitor with card so that you can select the colors you like.

3. An interactive system. Once text is put on the page, you must be able to edit it or move it around. This is more important with brochure layout but it is still very important when typesetting books. It is difficult, discouraging and time-consuming to have to switch back to the word processing mode to make changes.

4. A WYSIWYG (What You See Is What You Get) display so that we can always see what the page will look like. All the type, whether **bold**, *italic*, underscored or small caps, should be shown in proper size and style.

Microsoft-*Word* will not show the headlines in proper size. For that, you will need a page layout program. But *Word* does most everything else well.

5. There should not be any typesetting codes to clutter up the text on the screen unless requested. Some programs place a series of characters in the margin or even in the text, to indicate type style and size. These notations are very distracting.

6. The mouse and icon system make the word processing and typesetting fun and much easier to learn.

Hardware: The hardware must be from a company that is stable with a growing user base so that most software and peripherals will be available from it and other companies in the future. The IBM is the current industry standard. If you select IBM or a workalike, you can always add to it and it will retain its resale value longer. IBM workalikes are acceptable if from a stable, growing company with a large installed user base with local repair service. The machine must be 100% IBM compatible.

Software: You need a powerful, versatile word processing program, a font program and/or, a page layout program. For word processing, MS-*Word* is one of the most popular, drives the laser printer well and allows you to set type in inches, metric or typesetting measurements: picas and points.

The best deal in font software is *Laser Fonts* from SoftCraft. For about $270. you can produce two typefaces (Classic—similar to Times Roman and Sans Serif—similar to Helvetica) in 6 to 24 pt. in regular, **bold** and *italic*. For a brochure, write Soft-Craft, Inc., 16 North Carroll, Suite #500-P, Madison, WI 53703.

Rightwriter is a document proofreader and writing style analyzer. It checks manuscripts for errors in grammar, usage, spelling, punctuation and style. The cost is just $95. from Decisionware, 2033 Wood Street #218-B, Sarasota, FL 33577.

Printers: The Apple LaserWriter II-NT is the Cadillac of the industry. It has more memory, the *Postscript* page description language with several built-in typefaces and provides 300 dpi (dots per inch) for the whole page. The H-P LaserJet Series II is much less expensive and comes with two typefaces similar to Times-Roman and Helvetica.

If you have a book to typeset, buy a laser printer and you will pay for it with the money saved from traditional typesetting. If you do not need a laser printer yet, wait a few months. The prices are coming down, the standards are being set and there will be a shakeout in the industry. The longer you wait, the less expensive they will become.

How to buy: Make a list of what you want and visit local computer stores for bids. Most are discounting now. Deal locally so you can get service and help. Tell them you want the software loaded and the hardware up and running so all you have to do is take it home and plug it in. Loading the software and setting up the printer can be tricky and very time-consuming the first time. If you would like to know what hardware and software were used to typeset and layout this book, see the Colophon in the back.

Photocomposition type. Computerized books may be typeset with a laser printer or their disks may be taken to a typesetting shop for photocomposition output. Photocomposition type is sharper and clearer than laser output though few readers will notice. It is also more expensive since you will be passing your manuscript through another set of hands. See the *Yellow Pages* and call local shops and ask about their capabilities. These shops will provide you with a set of formatting codes which you will enter into the manuscript to indicate the typestyles desired.

If you don't type. If you cannot type, all is not lost. There are other ways to put your thoughts on paper.

Secretarial services. Secretarial services will work from handwritten copy or recorded dictation. Copy may be dictated into cassette recorders, including the small hand-held models, or even over the telephone. They will hook their telephone to their "tape tank" for later transcription. Most services use sophisticated computerized equipment and all work for much less than typesetters or graphic arts shops. Perhaps even more important, these services don't get upset over making revisions. See the *Yellow Pages* or ask your copy center to recommend local secretarial services.

A typical short-run book production cycle might look like this: you hand-write, typewrite or dictate your copy and give it to a secretarial service. It may be hand-carried locally or mailed to a distant firm. They enter your words into their machine, print out a double-spaced copy for your editing and file your disks. You mark up your printout with your corrections and send it back to them. They insert your disk into the word processor, flash your copy onto the screen, make the changes you have indicated and print out either another double-spaced correction copy or the single-spaced final page. You paste in your illustrations on the final copy and take the whole thing to your copy center for offset or xerographic reproduction.

When you want to update the book, you can call the service for a double-spaced printout or simply make changes in a present edition. Obviously, this is an ideal system for catalog work. The secretarial service will charge you only for the input time done by human beings and the very short machine-produced typesetting time. Another important advantage is that since the type is computer reproduced, you need only proof the *changes*. The rest of the copy will be exactly the same as the previous edition even though it has been moved around on the pages. It will also be very easy to change formats if, for example, you should wish to switch from 8.5 x 11 with two columns to 5.5 x 8.5 single column for the next edition. Simply push a couple of buttons and the printer will bang it out, camera-ready.

For straight copy (pages of type without artwork) the whole pasteup step is eliminated since the pages come out of the word processor's printer ready for the camera. This amounts to a great savings since many graphic arts shops charge as much to paste up a page as they do to set the type for it.

Secretarial services typically charge much less than typesetters and graphic arts shops. You will pay a little more for their word processing work than if you type the copy yourself but it will look better and later revisions will be much cheaper than typewriting.

Professionally set type. Having your type set will increase your costs though it may produce a product with a more professional appearance. The spacing between the letters will be proportional and the right-hand margin will be justified. The copy will fit into a smaller area through the use of smaller type and less space (called "leading," rhymes with "heading") between the lines. If you decide to have your type set, contact several local typesetters. While there, ask for a type specimen book so you can select the styles you like.

Hot type. The old typesetting systems used heavy lead characters: monotype and hot cast Linotype. These methods are limited in their versatility, are hard to find now and it is highly doubtful that you will use them.

Cold type. The two basic methods of setting cold type are typewriter-like strike-on and camera-like photocomposition. These may be thought of as a dry process and a wet process since photocomposition requires processing chemicals. The IBM Composer is the most common strike-on type machine. The photocomposition systems are computer-controlled, highly sophisticated and very expensive. Only printers and graphic arts shops can justify their purchase. One source of reconditioned IBM Composers is the Word Processing Exchange, 209 Main Street, Ann Arbor, MI 48108. Write for a catalog.

Editing. Secretarial services, copy shops and printers are not editors. Ordinarily they will correct some of the more obvious errors they see in the course of their work but if you ask them to edit, and they offer this service, it will cost extra. Computer programs will catch most spelling and punctuation errors, but not all.

"Editing" may range from spelling corrections, to rewriting, to design help. If you are concerned about content, send a copy to an expert in the field for "peer" review. Once the final draft is produced, it is always wise to have someone else proof the copy for spelling and punctuation. Texts for academic use and other manuals slated for periodic updating may carry a "change recommendation page" in the back to solicit corrections from users. Then the next edition will be even more useful and nearly error free. Keep the book's sales potential in mind; the greater the potential audience, the more time spent on editing.

Proofreading. Proofreading has to be done again and again. You will proof your manuscript for content and style and then will proof the book as it makes its way through the various stages of production. If you are producing your book utilizing a word processor and xerography, there will be less proofreading as some of the production steps are eliminated and only the changed areas need be proofed.

Proofreading marks. Proofreader's marks are standardized to help you communicate clearly with your typesetter or printer. A complete set can be found in your dictionary under "proofreader's marks."

ℰ or ૪ or ⁊	delete; take it out
◠	close up; print as one word
◠ꞌ	delete and close up
∧ or ⟩ or ⋏	caret; insert here ⟨something⟩
#	insert a space
eq #	space evenly where indicated
stet	let marked text stand as set
tr	transpose; change order the
/	used to separate two or more marks and often as a concluding stroke at the end of an insertion
[⌊	set farther to the left
] set⌋	farther to the right
⌢	set æ or fl as ligatures æ or fl
=	straighten alignment
∥ ∥	straighten or align
✗	imperfect or broken character
□	indent or insert em quad space
¶	begin a new paragraph
(SP)	spell out ⟨set 5 lbs. as five pounds⟩
cap	set in capitals ⟨CAPITALS⟩
sm cap or s.c.	set in small capitals ⟨SMALL CAPITALS⟩
lc	set in lowercase ⟨lowercase⟩
ital	set in italic ⟨italic⟩
rom	set in roman ⟨roman⟩
bf	set in boldface ⟨boldface⟩
= or -/ or ◠ or /Ħ/	hyphen
$\frac{1}{N}$ or eℛ or /N/	en dash ⟨1965-72⟩
$\frac{1}{M}$ or em or /M/	em — or long — dash
∨	superscript or superior ⟨as in πr^2⟩
∧	subscript or inferior ⟨as in H_2O⟩
◇ or ✕	centered ⟨for a centered dot in $p \cdot q$⟩
⌒	comma
∨	apostrophe
⊙	period
; or ;/	semicolon
: or ⊙	colon
❝❞ or ✓✓	quotation marks
(/)	parentheses
[/]	brackets
QK/?	query to author: has this been set as intended?
⊥ or ⊥¹	push down a work-up
⑨¹	turn over an inverted letter
wf¹	wrong font; a character of the wrong size or esp. style

Proofreader's Marks

Previously printed copy. Since your book will be reproduced via a photographic process, most any previously printed material may be used. For example, if you wish to include one of your previously published magazine articles, it may be pasted in. There is no need to retype it. However, there will probably be a difference in the typestyles used in your book and in the magazine and you will have to decide whether this detracts from the quality of your finished product. Photocopied articles reprint well if they have good contrast. By adjusting the machines density control, you will make the print as dark as possible without turning the white background to gray.

Headlines. Headlines such as chapter titles are produced with display type. You may set your own using dry transfer rub-on letters or acetate lift off letters available at most stationers and graphic arts stores, or you may patronize a printer or graphic arts shop with a headliner machine.

1. Dry transfer type is rubbed on, or "burnished," from a carrier sheet.

2. The lift off type is printed on a clear plastic sheet with an adhesive backing. It is cut out and positioned in place.

3. Headliner machines normally use a photographic process to produce large type in a line. This method is faster but more expensive.

4. If you are using a computer with a laser printer, you will set headlines along with the type. All four

approaches provide a large range of type styles and sizes.

**Transfer type is available in a
large variety of styles and sizes.**

6 Helvetica
7 Helvetica
8 Helvetica
8½ Helvetica
9 Helvetica
10 Helvetica
11 Helvetica
12 Helvetica
13 Helvetica
14 Helvetica
15 Helvetica
16 Helvetica
17 Helvetica
18 Helvetica
19 Helvetica
20 Helvetica
21 Helvetica
22 Helvetica
23 Helvetica
24 Helvetica

**Letter height is measured in "points."
There are 72 points to the inch.**

Transfer (rub on) type is easy to use. Complete instructions may be obtained when you buy the type. The lift off type found in the Formatt catalog may prove to be even easier to work with.

1. CUT LIGHTLY and SLIDE knifeblade under letter. 2. PRESS letter to blade and LIFT off backing sheet. 3. To position, place guideline under letter over guideline on artwork and smooth into place with finger. 4. Trim away guideline and BURNISH FIRMLY.

Formatt brand lift off letters

Artwork. While artwork is not required in all publications, a certain number of drawings, borders, arrows, etc. will certainly dress them up. Some books are simply not complete without charts and graphs.

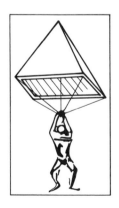

Line drawing

Extra lines were crowded into this line drawing to give it an appearance of shading

Artwork consists of line drawings and halftones. Line work is a clean black-on-white drawing without any shading. Unless it must be camera-enlarged or reduced, a line drawing may be pasted directly on the page, since it can be reproduced along with the typed copy without further treatment. Drawings are recommended wherever possible because they do not require the additional expensive manufacturing steps of photographs.

Drawings should be made with a hard, fine-point felt tip pen with black ink on a high quality, smooth white paper. Be sure the ink does not bleed on the paper or creep under the rule by testing the pen first. Experiment by reducing oversize drawings on a photocopier. Often photos may be traced with good results.

Shaded effects may be achieved by crowding or cross-hatching fine lines. Remember, the camera will only pick up lines, not shades of gray.

It is safer to make your drawings on separate sheets of paper for pasting onto the final sheet. This makes the occasional mistake less painful, although errors may be covered over with white opaquing liquid.

For those who cannot draw or even trace, there are commercial artists. Check the *Yellow Pages*, ask at the local quick print shop for a recommendation or contact a nearby college art department.

Clip art. "Clip Art" is sold by the book or sheet and consists of line drawings on almost every possible subject. It lacks originality but it is less expensive than hiring an artist. Clip art may be available from your local graphic arts shop or college bookstore. Your quick print shop should be able to tell you where to find clip art catalogs and they may have a selection of them right there in their own file. See the Appendix for addresses of clip art publishers.

Examples of clip art

Other sources of art. Art may be taken from old magazines or books. If the copyright has expired, the illustrations are in the public domain. Prior to January 1, 1978, copyright protection was for 28 years and was renewable for another 28 years. Therefore, anything printed prior to 1932 is safe and anything in print prior to 1960 is probably safe. The steel engravings found in many old publications are often nice and reproduce very well.

Depending upon your subject, you may be able to clip drawings from certain newer military and government publications. Such art, paid for by the taxpayers, is also in the public domain.

Graphic aids. Display symbols, borders and shading mediums are used just like display type.

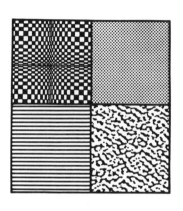

Shading mediums   **Sample use**

Lines and borders   **Symbols and ornaments**

Reductions. Quite often the drawings we wish to use are too large and must be reduced to fit properly on the page. Reductions are usually sharper than the original since the lines become crowded closer together. The least expensive way to reduce line drawings is on a photocopy machine. Some photocopy machines will reduce to 98%, 74% or 65%

and will handle originals up to 11" x 17." Other machines have variable reduction capability. Call the nearby copy shops and ask what their equipment can do.

Most printers have camera equipment which will duplicate your artwork in the same, enlarged or reduced size. These photostats (or veloxes) cost more than xerography, but they are very clean.

Whole pages of type and drawings may also be reduced for economics of space, but the entire page must be reduced the same amount. Both **height** and **width** will be reduced in the same proportions. For example, when copy is reduced to half its height, it also shrinks to half its width.

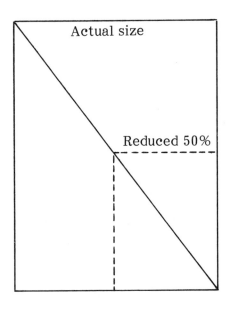

Actual size

Reduced 50%

Scaling grid

Tracing each order back to a specific promotional effort or paid ad is important business intelligence. Without this information, you may be unknowingly spending your energy and money in the wrong plac₍ when you continue because you don't k are paying off by b₁ your time and mone₅ them in those place₅ return.

Tracing each order back to a specific promotional effort or paid ad is important business intelligence. Without this information, you may be unknowingly spending your energy and money in the wrong places. Waste becomes tragedy when you continue blind promotional spending because you don't know for sure which projects are paying off by bringing in book orders. Both your time and money are limited, you must spend them in those places which will bring maximum return.

Example of a 74% reduction

The reduction of an occasional illustration can be very useful and the price is easily justified by the space saved. On the other hand, reducing whole pages of type can be terribly confusing and is not recommended to the novice. For more discussion of reductions, see Chapter Four.

Photographs. The offset printing press process can only distinguish between black and non-black areas. Images with shading, such as photographs, require an extra step to make them acceptably reproducible. The process is called "screening" and the product of the screening is a "halftone."

Halftones are made from photographs, or drawings with shading, by taking a photograph of them through a screen. You will notice the result using a loupe or magnifying glass to look closely at a printed photograph. Halftones are composed of many tiny dots of various sizes but the eye runs the dots together so the areas appear shaded. Screening requires camera work and the extra service costs five to eight dollars each. The cost is not great when spread out over a large press run but photos are more work than line drawings.

85 line

100 line

120 line

Screens come in several values and are measured in dots per linear inch. The more dots, the crisper the printed halftone. Newspapers commonly use a 65- or 85- line screen (65 or 85 dots per running inch) while books are commonly done in 120-, 133- or even 150-line.

Many quick print shops specializing in instant printing are limited to a 100-line screen as they employ a special system which shoots the copy directly onto the thin paper printing plate, bypassing the negative stage. If you want a finer screen, they'll have to make a metal plate. Metal plates require a process camera which they may not have; the work must be subcontracted. All this will add to your start-up costs. If you must use a metal plate, try to concentrate the photos on a single page. Print the rest of the pages with paper plates, or xerography.

Photos taken from other magazines and books have already been screened and may be pasted right onto the boards. Usually they have been screened to 133-lines, which is not acceptable to paper plates without loss of quality. If the photos are to be enlarged or reduced, they must be re-screened and this usually reduces their quality.

With both photos and drawings, reductions are preferable to enlargements. Reductions become sharper while enlargements only magnify flaws, losing clarity.

Reductions should be limited to 45% of the original size and enlargements to 150% as these are the single-step plate making limits of many cameras.

Black-and-white shots screen best. Unless very sharp, color photographs tend to become muddy when printed in black and white. Red appears to be black to the camera while blue is reproduced as white. Unless you are publishing an art-type book, you will use black and white rather than the much more expensive color photos. Color requires four trips through the press plus prepress "color separations."

The best photos are large (they become sharper when reduced), glossy, black and white with a lot of contrast. If you must work from color, have a local photolab make a black-and-white print from your color print or transparency. You will be able to see what you can expect from it once printed and you may then proceed to have it screened like any other black-and-white photo.

Start with good photographs, sharp and with good contrast. Every time illustrations go through the camera they lose a little quality. The finished printed product is rarely as good as the original photograph.

Crop marks should be made on the margins of the photo. Do not scribe lines across it. For the process camera (negative and metal plate), the marks should be made in red or black ink. For xerography or photo direct plates (paper or plastic), use a light blue pen. Do not connect the lines of the crop marks or their corners will appear in the printed photograph. Remember, if you reduce the height of an illustration, the camera will also reduce the width proportionally. Do not write on the back of a photo; attach your instructions to it with tape.

There are five ways to prepare photographs for short-run printing. The one you choose will depend on the quality required, price and the availability of local services.

1. Photomechanical transfer (PMT) is a photographic process which produces a screened positive print bypassing the negative stage. Common PMT screens are 65-, 85-, 100-, 110-, 120- and 133-line. PMTs will fade in time; they do not last as long as veloxes. For information on PMTs, write Eastman Kodak Co., Graphic Marketing Division, Rochester, NY 14650 and request a copy of *Copy Preparation Using PMT Materials* (Q-71).

2. A velox is a screened print made in two steps via a photographic negative. Some imperfections may be opaqued (blotted out) on the negative, the print lasts longer and it may cost slightly more than a PMT. The velox may be pasted on the layout board.

3. A copyscreen may be used when you are in a hurry and high quality is not required. Simply cut the screen to the size of the photo and paste both onto the board. Graphic Products Corporation produces an 85-line model called "Copyscreen-2." The 9" x 12.5" screen sells for about $3 so this method is actually cheaper than making a PMT or velox.

4. Some Polaroid cameras may be fitted with a screen so that their 4" x 5" prints come out as halftones ready to be trimmed to size and pasted to the board. This system is popular with real estate people who want to make up instant flyers on their new homes. The screen kits are available in 65-, 85- and 100-line and will fit all Polaroid film packs or roll type black-and-white film. Check with a camera store for this camera accessory or write The Printers Shopper, 111-P Press Lane, Chula Vista, CA 92010.

5. The standard way is to photographically shoot a screened negative of the original photographic print and then to strip the negative into the line negative or "flat" for burning onto the metal printing plate. This method provides the best quality, especially when a fine tone screen (e.g., 133-line) is used. Use this method for long print runs.

Photos will be screened and reproduced as negatives or positive prints. Negatives are normally used in offset printing while copyscreens, PMTs and veloxes may be pasted right on your copy and run through the photocopy machine. Many new publishers like these methods best as they can see what they are going to get as they paste up their book.

Do not build your book around the photographs. As the manuscript is composed, make a list of the required photos. Then borrow, buy or take them yourself. The exception might be a book on photographs but then you would be using fancy and expensive, not short-run, printing techniques.

Using the photocopy machine. The second part of the small book production revolution (the first is the computer/laser typesetter) is the new photocopy machines which reproduce photographs fairly well. With them, the printing press and all the setup time are eliminated. These machines will also faithfully reproduce large areas of solid black such as fat block letters. The results still are not as good as offset press work with a metal plate but the method is faster and cheaper for short-run production.

In many ways, xerography is much more versatile than offset printing. Before running each page, test copies may be made while varying the density setting. This will allow you to achieve dark print without picking up the edges of the pasted-down material. Unwanted specks may be eliminated by applying white opaquing liquid to the offending area on the original. Xerography seems to reproduce 100-line halftones best.

Perhaps you can't *tell* but you can *sell* a book by its cover, and color sells. You may elect to have your cover offset printed in color or a photocopy machine may be used on color cover stock. If you are running just a few covers, you might try the new color copiers. Call the nearest copier sales offices listed in the *Yellow Pages* and go in for a demonstration or ask them who has one nearby. There aren't many color copiers and they may be difficult to locate. These machines do a fairly good job from color slides and some artwork. Run some tests.

Reproducible copy. Your copy is "camera-ready" if it is ready to be printed with no further pasteup work. Good copies will only result from good originals. This means sharp black images (words, drawings, clip art, charts, screened photos) on smooth white paper with adequate margins on all four sides. If the images are not a dense black, the camera will reproduce them in a thin, uneven and broken manner. Rough paper will produce an uneven image while colored paper will result in background shadows. Both photocopy and offset machines require margins, they need an edge to grip. Your book will not look professional without adequate margins and at least 3/8" is required on the inside (e.g., left margin of a right-hand page) so that copy will not get lost in the bound edge or "gutter."

The camera sees anything black on a white back ground. But light blue appears white to the camera while red looks black. This is why some dark areas of artwork are sometimes covered with a red film and notes are written with a special light blue editing pencil. When pasting existing articles and other outside work into your finished copy, beware of the following:

1. Red, magenta, purple and orange will come out black. If your piece has black print on a red background it will come out as a solid black patch.

2. Blue, green and yellow will not be noticed by the camera, especially if light. Signatures should be made in red or black ink, do not use a blue ink pen.

3. Black or red ink on dark colored paper will turn out muddy.

4. Orange, green and brown will not be picked up by the camera when printed on a colored background.

5. Red ink on light pink or orange paper will not reproduce well. When in doubt, run a test.

Use thin or outline lettering

Offset presses and some of the new photocopiers will handle large solid black areas such as block letters but many copy machines will not. For most photocopiers it is best to use outline letters rather than block type for heads. If you are not sure about a piece of copy or artwork, run a test.

Chapter Four

Layout and Pasteup

*L*ayout is the design of the artwork and typed copy on the page while *pasteup* consists of the physical application of the type, artwork, photographs or other dressing to that page. If your book consists entirely of previously published magazine articles, then the layout is done. In fact, the articles may not even have to be pasted up.

The objective is to paste up each page completely yourself so that all the quick print shop has to do is to place them in their machine. This provides you with the least expensive approach as well as the maximum control over the finished product. The simplified system outlined in this chapter will allow you to keep all the elements of a page on one sheet of paper. There will not be any extra pieces to get lost. You will achieve full visualization of each page prior to printing. Last minute corrections and changes will be easier and cheaper. All preparatory materials will belong to you, not to the printer.

Do not try to be too fancy on your first project. Be practical and concentrate on the content. Present your information well. On the next job, after you understand the capabilities of the systems, you may be more creative in layout.

The simplest form of layout consists of ordinary typing on a regular 8.5 x 11 sheet of paper. All you have to remember is to stay within the margins. Word processors may also be used in this way and they provide the added advantage of professional-appearing typeset copy. In the following pages we will outline a simplified form of layout and pasteup. Even if you are planning to publish straight text, you should have an understanding of all the possibilities—the whole picture.

Layout area. The workspace must be clean and kept clean. Offices and bedrooms are preferred to kitchens for this type of work. There will be a lot of important little pieces of paper which can easily become lost or damaged.

Tools and supplies. All that is absolutely necessary is a jar of rubber cement, a T square, and a smooth surface with a straight edge on one side, such as a table. However, other tools and supplies will make your job easier and more fun. All are available at art supply stores, most stationery stores, many college book stores and some quick print shops. See the Appendix for catalogs of pasteup supplies.

Drawing board. A standard wood drawing board measuring 18" x 24" with plain edges will do the job and is relatively inexpensive. However, if all your pasteup work will be on 8.5" x 11" paper, you might like a more compact 12" x 16" piece of 1/4" plastic.

Light table. If most of your reproduction will be on an automatic feed xerographic machine you may prefer a more expensive light table to a drawing board. A light table is a thin rectangular box with a glass top and a light inside. Page outlines may be scribed on the glass once rather than repeatedly on the pasteup boards. This is quite a time saver. Temporary light tables are easy and inexpensive to make. Fit a cut down cardboard box with a small, self-contained under–counter type fluorescent light and lay a sheet of 1/4" clear plastic over the top. Make the margin outlines on the plastic with thin black border tape. Now with a T square and a triangle, you are in business.

T square. The T square must be large enough to match the drawing board.

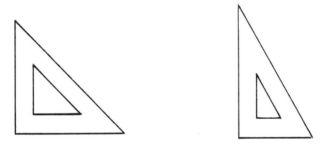

Triangles. You will need one 12" long 30-60 degree triangle and one 8" 45-90 model. Both are plastic.

Scissors. Most any good scissors will do, but some commercial artists like barber's shears best while others prefer large paper-hanging shears for some jobs.

Knife. A razor-sharp X-Acto blade-type knife is required.

Pens. For black lines, professionals use Rapidograph pens which are rather temperamental. Most of us can get by more cheaply and easily with a fine point, hard felt tip pen or a fine tip ball point.

Non-repro blue is available in both pencil and felt tip pen form and the pen is easy to use. Notes and guide lines drawn in light blue will not be picked up by the camera.

Ruler/straight edge. A metal ruler/straight edge is preferable to less durable plastic. The plastic edge may be nicked when using the straight edge as a cutting guide for a knife.

Paper. Type is usually set on paper which is then cut up and pasted on heavier stock. It must be a paper which will accept ink without running. Good ones are 28 lb. or 32 lb. sulphite or rag ledger and 70 lb. or 80 lb. offset book paper.

The paper must not be too thick or the pasted up elements will produce shadows around their edges and these edges will show up as lines in the printed work. In the more expensive regular printing methods utilizing a negative, these lines may be covered on the negative with dark opaquing fluid. In the less expensive direct plate method, edges of the original pasted-up board may be touched up with white opaquing fluid and the density control of the xerography machine or plate maker may be adjusted. If the pasted element is very thick, the density control must be moved so far toward the "light" setting that the type may begin to break up.

Any smooth white paper will do, but the best results are obtained on "repro" typesetting paper, a clay coated hard surfaced white paper with a coated back to resist curl. "Matte" paper has a smooth, even surface and is free from shine. Do not use erasable bond which has a tendency to smear and blur with handling. When in doubt, run tests using different papers, ribbons and impression controls; inspect the characters with a loupe or magnifying glass. Show the samples to your printer and get his or her approval before you set your type.

Repro paper is often hard to find. In fact, when questioned many paper dealers and graphic arts shops will give you a blank stare. One manufacturer is Zellerbach and one retail source is Dot Pasteup Supply Co., P.O. Box 369-P, Omaha, NE 68101. Send $1 (refundable) for their catalog. Another source is IBM. Call (800) 631-5582 and ask for Photo-Master paper #1136296. 500 sheets of this 8.5 x 11 paper runs about $45.

Rubber cement. Rubber cement is the only glue which should be used to paste up artwork. Most other glues will wrinkle the paper or lose their flexibility. Rubber cement stays wet momentarily, allowing the copy to be positioned. Excess cement can be removed from the edges simply by rubbing it off. Keep the top on the jar between uses to prolong the life of the cement.

A simple small jar of rubber cement will do for most jobs. If you find you are doing a lot of pasteup work, you may wish to invest in a rubber cement pot with a height adjustable brush. They load just the with a height adjustable brush. They load just the tip of the brush with cement. By now you will be buying your rubber cement in larger cans and will want to pick up some thinner too.

Be sure to remove all the excess glue from around the edges of each pasted element or the glue will print as a pasteup line.

Rubber cemented artwork may be removed by squirting rubber cement thinner under the artwork.

A "rubber cement pickup" is a stiff little sponge that removes the extra cement which leaks out from under the pasted artwork. You can make your own pickup by allowing some rubber cement to dry out or by collecting some old pieces into a ball.

Wax. Professionals use a machine to coat the back of the artwork with hot wax. The wax does not adhere as strongly as rubber cement so artwork may be lifted and repositioned even after the wax has cooled (but sometimes important little pieces fall off and get lost.) The machines require a long warm up time and are expensive so they are not of particular interest for occasional pasteup work.

A small no-heat waxer in the style of a lipstick or glue stick is available from Jiffy Printers Products, 1095 Coronet Avenue, Pasadena, CA 91107.

Never use transparent tape to attach artwork to the pasteup board. The camera will pick it up. Spray adhesives are available for pasteup work but they are expensive and can be messy. If you do choose a spray adhesive, select the removable type, not the permanent. Apply a very thin "mist" coat for best results.

White opaquing liquid. These fluids are useful for covering drawing and composition errors. They may also be used to mask edges of artwork which will otherwise appear to be a line to the camera. These fluids tend to dry out and become worthless. Some printers say the Xerox brand is both the best and the least expensive. To improve masters for photocopying, use the special white opaquing liquid developed "for copies." For correcting line drawings, use the liquid developed for "pen & ink".

Miscellaneous supplies. You will also want to consider a burnishing tool for pressing transfer type and other artwork to the board, drafting tape (like masking tape but it remains pliable) to secure your work to the drafting board, clear spray to protect important artwork from smudging, tweezers for handling small elements, white tape for coverups and a proportional scale for figuring enlargements and reductions. Check the displays and catalogs at your local art supply store. While you are there, look into their variety of transfer type and clip art.

Selecting book size. Considering the book size and binding discussions in Chapter Two, select the format (size) you want for your book. Since the human eye has trained on narrow columns such as those found in newspapers, it is normal to choose a two-column format for wide pages.

Most xerography machines will copy on 8.5 x 11 and 8.5 x 14 paper. The larger "legal" size paper may prove useful for certain applications. Folded, the pages will measure 8.5" high and 7" wide.

MARGIN GUIDE for 5½" X 8½" books produced on 8½" x 11" paper. These measurements may also be used for 8½" X 7" books made from legal size 8½" x 14" paper; the working area will be larger but the margins will remain the same.

Adjoining pages should be pasted up on these sheets just as they will appear in the final copy. However, before they are taken to the copy center, they will have to be separated (cut) down the center and mated with other pages. More on this later in this chapter.

Center

An even-numbered page

All copy must fit within these lines.

Allow 1" in the "gutter" for saddle stitching and 1½" for perfect binding

½" for perfect binding and 3/4" for saddle stitching.
Some of this area may be trimmed off after binding.

An odd-numbered page

MARGIN GUIDE for 8½" x 11" books produced on 8½" x 11" paper. These measurements may also be used for 8½" x 14" books made from legal size paper; the working areas will be larger but the margins will remain the same.

You may fit your text in one column to full width if the lines of type have a lot of space between them. Single spaced typewriter type should be set two columns to the page.

½" Top margin

Center

5/8"

All copy must fit within these lines.

¼"

5/8" Bottom margin

Many quick print shops have 11 x 17 offset presses which can produce saddle-stitched (folded, with wire staples in the spine) 8.5 x 11 books, but this is much more expensive for short runs. Offset printing requires extra plate-making steps, and there is more setup time.

Here we will concentrate on standard 8.5 x 11 and 5.5 x 8.5 books which may be most economically produced in short runs by xerography and direct plate methods. You can always get fancier and pay more.

Sheets vs. page. A sheet of paper has two sides and each side is a page. Inexpensive short-run book printing will be done through a xerographic process in copy shops on 8.5 x 11 paper. One sheet of this paper will yield two pages (one on each side) in an 8.5 x 11 format book and four pages in a 5.5 x 8.5 format book.

Page makeup for straight copy. If you are not planning a fancy layout or artwork, you can eliminate the pasteup sequence by setting the typing margins so that the type will fall within the margin guides shown in the examples. Simply type your copy on 8.5 x 11 repro paper. The only measurements you will have to make will be to locate the page numbers. If you are using a word processor, even this function is automatic. Page numbers should fall back to back to minimize see-through in the final book.

Incidentally, the ratio of double-spaced ten-pitch typewriter copy on an 8.5 x 11 sheet of paper to single-spaced twelve-pitch typewriter copy in a 5.5 x 8.5 book page is about one to one. This comparison may be helpful in projecting book size from a raw manuscript.

Page makeup for type and artwork. There are two basic ways to make the pasteup: on stiff cardboard with a drawing board or on a sheet of paper with a light table. Boards are the professional way common to the industry. They are more durable and may be best if you are pasting up many small elements. On the other hand, this method is more expensive, the boards will not feed through a photocopy machine automatically and they require more time for margin scribing.

When pasting up on paper, margins may be outlined on the light table or on a clear plastic sheet taped to the glass. We will discuss both the drawing board and the light table methods.

Pasteup board. Professionals use commercial illustration board, but plain white flexible bristol board will do as well. Commercial board has (nonreproducing) light blue lines to aid in copy layout. Check your local art supply store and see the Appendix for art supply catalogs.

Preparing the boards—light table. Light tables should be used when pasting up for xerographic or direct plate reproduction as they eliminate the need for ruling each pasteup board.

Light tables are available in various sizes and they are very easy to make. Visit a graphic arts store to view one up close. Easy rush jobs may even be done on the "infinite depth, vertical, solar-powered light box" found in most rooms: the window.

Start by making a pasteup guide on a clear plastic sheet. The markings may be placed directly on the glass of the light box but done on a plastic sheet, the marks may be easily changed, removed and installed. Use thin black border tape to make the margin guides, trim marks and page number indicator.

Some people like to use graph paper-like layout paper which has light blue guide lines. A bit of shopping may be required to find graph paper with the required lines because there is a wide variety. Check artist supply stores and catalogs.

Pasteup work may be done on any white sheet such as 20 lb. mimeo or ordinary typing paper. Anchor the paper to the light table with tape. All the guide lines will show through. Now just paste in the elements.

Lay out the pages two at a time as they will appear in the book with even pages on the left and odd pages on the right. If there is a chart flowing from one page to the next, you will be able to visualize it in its printed form.

Number each page in the lower right-hand corner with a non-repro blue pen starting from number one. These numbers may not correspond to the book's page numbers. The printer will need these light blue numbers when he cuts the boards in two and reassembles them for printing.

Preparing the boards—drafting board. If you are planning on longer print runs, your printer may choose to use a process camera, negatives and metal plates. In this case, you may paste up the pages in the normal manner using a drafting board.

Before you begin to lay out a major project, paste up a couple of sample pages and take them to your copy shop for a critique. Run a few xerographic copies to see how you are doing as a neophyte graphic artist.

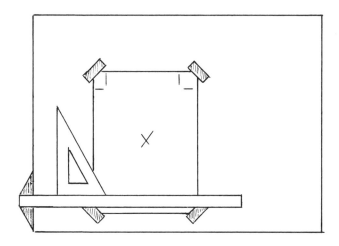

Place a piece of white pasteup board on your drafting board and anchor it with tape. Mark the center with a non-repro blue pencil or pen. The easiest way to locate the center is to place a ruler diagonally— from corner to corner and make small marks halfway.

Measure 4.25" to each side of the center mark and 5.5" above and below it. Then with the T square and triangle, use black ink to draw two lines or "trim marks" in each corner of the sheet, outside the job area. Now you can see the limits of your 8.5 x 11 page. This is how the professionals do it and if you should decide to print your book using regular high speed techniques, the printer will use these marks for positioning the negatives in the flats.

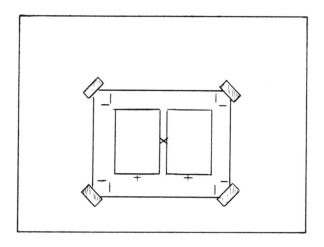

Now, using the non-repro blue pen or pencil, draw in the margin guides. All these lines will be more accurate if the measurements are made off the center mark.

Trim marks. An easy way to scribe the trim marks is with a reversible template.

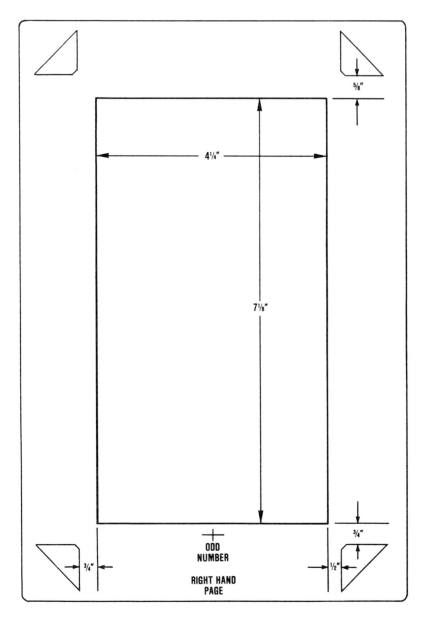

5/8"

4¼"

7⅛"

3/4"

ODD
NUMBER

3/4"

½"

RIGHT HAND
PAGE

Reversible trim mark template for 5.5 x 8.5 pages

Note that the reversible clear plastic template is offset to one side. By using one side for right-hand, odd-numbered pages and the flip side for left-hand, even-numbered pages, wider margins are provided in the center or "gutter" of the book.

To make the above described template, use overhead projector pens with permanent ink. One brand is Vis-a-Vis from Sanford.

The four elements of a pasteup. You may use any or all of the four basic elements of a pasteup on a given page.

1. **Type** includes headlines, text, captions, signatures, etc.

2. **Artwork** consists of line drawings, clip art, etc.

3. **Photographs**, as is or retouched, are self- explanatory.

4. **Dressing** is ornamentation such as arrows, symbols, rules, and borders.

Each element must be carefully positioned to fit on the page prior to pasting down.

Positioning the elements. Cut out each of the elements, trying to leave a one-eighth inch border around the edges. Make the cuts as straight and even as possible. Place the elements on the board so you can visualize them in their final position. Most people like to make their transfer-type headlines on a separate sheet of paper. If you are doing a short booklet or the chapters have just a few pages, you may wish to make a rough layout on several sheets of plain paper before transferring them to the final board. Using a non-repro blue pencil, mark the position of each element.

Next, ruled lines and borders should be inked-in directly on the board. Then wait until the work is completely dry.

Select and trim an appropriate amount of text, check it for fit, place it face down on a clean sheet of paper and apply rubber cement to all but the very edges of the underside. Place the glued text on the board, staying within the guidelines. Line up the left margin of the text with the vertical blue guideline. This may be "eyeballed" but it will be easier and straighter if the T square and triangle are used. Elements will slide for positioning while the rubber cement is still wet. Use the tip of your knife to move the smaller pieces.

Now, working from the top down, put each of the other elements in place. Use a T square to make sure they are straight. Overlay a clean sheet of paper to burnish the elements; rub over the paper to glue them down.

Mark the page numbers in non-repro blue for the time being unless the word processor has already put them in place. Typed or typeset numbers may be added later, when you are sure what they will be.

Watch the hands of a graphic artist. They use the knife blade rather than their fingers to pick up and position pasteup elements.

Corrections. Minor errors may be scraped off the pasteup with the knife. Larger problems will require opaquing fluid or white art tape.

New corrected text may be pasted right over the error. Corrections tend to be straighter if you paste over the whole line rather than just individual words. Trim the new copy carefully to make sure it does not cover the edge of other good copy.

Solvent. Rubber cement is quite volatile and it firms up after continued exposure to the air. Keep the cap on! Thinner may be used to bring the cement back to proper consistency, but if made too thin, the cement will not stick. Thinner may also be used to remove pasted elements. Squirt it under the stuck piece as you gently lift the artwork from the board. The volatile thinner dries quickly without staining. Use a "pickup" eraser to remove the residual cement. Avoid breathing the vapors as well as skin contact with the solvent.

Borders and bleeds. Always keep the copy within the borders outlined by the margin guides. Do not allow it to bleed, or extend to the edge of the page. The book will be much more attractive if laid out properly, according to convention.

Some room at one margin, usually 3/8", must be left for "grip area" so that the photocopier or offset press may pull the paper through. Depending upon the model of the machine, this grip area may be on the side or top of the paper. Check with the quick print shop before pasting up artwork.

Illustrations. Photos, artwork and charts should be pasted down straight across the page above and below the text. See the photographs in this book as an example. Keep it simple. Text can be fitted around the illustrations but this requires extra design time and a trip back to the typesetting machine or typewriter. The space saved by copy fitting is rarely justified by the effort required. On a two-column page, illustrations may be laid out either one column or two columns wide.

Photographs. Photographs require special handling, as discussed in Chapter Three. Each way of handling has its own peculiarities of cost, time required and result.

Photos must be screened if they are to reproduce properly and the screening may result in a positive print "velox" or in a negative film form. The velox looks just like a photograph but the images are now made up of tiny dots (half tone) instead of their usual continuous tone. If your quick print shop cannot screen the photos for you, they will tell you where it can be done locally.

In a lengthy book with a lot of photographs, you may wish to use veloxes since veloxes pasted on boards will be easier to proof. Another advantage is that the printer will not be able to lose a photograph or print it upside-down.

Depending upon the printing equipment to be used, there are several ways to reproduce photographs.

1. Xerography:
A. 100-line velox.
B. 100-line PMT.
C. 85-line copyscreen overlay.
D. 100-line Polaroid print.

2. Direct image paper plate:
A. 100-line velox.
B. 100-line PMT.
C. 85-line copyscreen overlay.
D. 100-line Polaroid print.

3. Metal plate:
A. 100-line velox.
B. 100-line PMT.
C. Normal negative method in 133-line.

If the book has just a few important photos and you want to make a short print run, you may choose to print the pages with photos with metal plates while doing the rest of the pages with xerography. Metal plates allow a much finer screen and produce much better detail in photographs.

In pasting up for metal plate work, you will fit each photo and paste a red film "rubylith" material on the board where you want the photo to fit. The printer will take the photograph separately and will make a screened negative from it to paste onto the flat. Do not paste the unscreened photo on the board. They are hard to remove and may be damaged. Check with your printer for details.

Where photos are given to the printer separately, be sure they are marked on the back with page number and position as well as size. Use a fine tip felt pen or a soft lead pencil and write near the edge of the photo so as not to score the surface.

When a photograph is being screened, it may be enlarged or reduced. See the discussion which follows.

Reductions. Any material may be enlarged or reduced photographically. The only limitation is that the size of photographs can be changed only before or during screening. If enlarged or reduced after screening, the dot size and resolution will change too.

Type and line drawings may be handled in either of two ways:

1. They can be set and pasted up oversize for reduction, or

2. They can be set, reduced on the photocopy machine or with the printer's more sophisticated equipment, and pasted up. This second method is usually easier for the neophyte pasteup artist to understand. The only drawback with this system is that the end result is not quite as sharp as the first alternative because the work has made an extra trip through the camera.

As mentioned above, photos must be handled separately. Treat them according to the photo discussions earlier. The mechanics of their enlargement and reduction are generally the same as for written copy. Some specific details follow.

Graphic Products Corporation makes a nice proportioning scale called a Computagrid which makes reductions easy to visualize. See the pasteup supply catalogs listed in the Appendix.

Remember, when you reduce the width, you also reduce the height. Outline your original and desired page sizes and draw a diagonal line as shown above to better understand the relationship.

If you are using a photocopier with a standard 74% reduction capability, simply set your type 135% larger than you want it to finally appear. For example, if your book has 4.25" x 7.125" columns, multiply 4.25 and 7.125 by 1.35 and set your type 5.74 by 9.62 inches. Then before you set too much type, take a page and run it through the machine to test your figures. And while you are at the quick print shop, it won't hurt to get a pasteup critique.

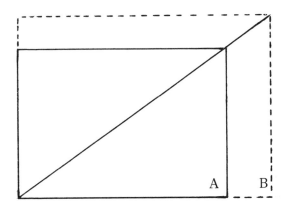

Method I: A is finished size and B is pasteup size.

**Method 2: A is both the pasteup and finished sizes and
B is the composition size.**

If copy and drawings can be reduced, it stands to reason that they can also be enlarged. While enlargements may lose some definition, the technique does come in handy at times.

Enlargements and reductions may be figured on a sheet of paper with a diagonal line or on a "proportion wheel" available at most graphic art supply stores. Proportion wheels read in both inches and percent. Enlargements and reductions are specified in percentages since they adjust in both height and width at the same time. Photos or copy begin at 100% of size and changes are specified from there. For example, if a photo is to be reduced 30%, then the reduction is specified as "70%" (of original size). And if it is to be enlarged 20%, the enlargement is specified as "120%."

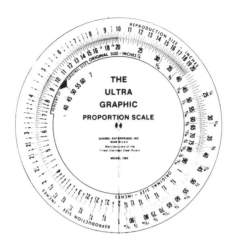

Proportion scale

Finishing the pasteup. Use a rubber cement pickup eraser to clean the cement around the edges of the typed or artwork elements. White opaquing liquid may be used to cover over any unwanted marks. Some people like to use a pointed No. 1 brush for this. Place a clean piece of paper over the pasted board and burnish the work. Rub the whole area with a burnisher or a rounded tool such as a soup spoon. Place a clean sheet of thin paper over the work and apply a couple of clear tape "hinges" to the top. This slip sheet will protect the work as you stack other pages on top. Then place the work in a clean storage area, clean up the work area and start on the next page.

Making a dummy of your book. You may wish to make up a dummy of your book so that you will be able to visualize the pages in relation to each other. It is customary to begin new chapters on the right-hand side and since not all chapters will end on a left-hand page, there may be some blanks. Only after the dummy is made will you be able to assign final page numbers. The dummy is comparatively simple for 8.5 x 11 formats and a little more difficult to understand for 5.5 x 8.5.

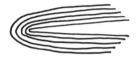

End view of dummy.

For a 5.5 x 8.5 book, count your boards and take one-quarter the number of 8.5 x 11 sheets of paper and fold them over. This will represent your book since you will be getting four pages to the sheet.

Last	1st		2nd	Next to last	
3rd from last	3rd		4th	4th from last	etc.

Signature layout

Now photocopy your boards and make a rough layout by pasting or taping the copy into the dummy. There will probably be some blank pages and you should adjust them to fall on the left-hand pages at the end of the chapters. Number the pages in the dummy and then renumber the corresponding boards.

Unfolding the dummy, you will find the last page (which could be blank) next to the first. Using the dummy as a guide, carefully cut the pasted up boards in half and rejoin them side by side in this new order.

Try to avoid completely blank pages. There is less chance for printer error and your customer will not complain of receiving an apparently defective book. Add an illustration or at least a page number.

If you do not make a dummy, be very careful in numbering the pages and include blank boards for blank pages. The printer must know what is to go on every page to get them in the right order.

Cover. The front and back covers may be laid out just like the interior pages. Lay them out side-by-side and leave some room in the center for the spine. The width of the spine will depend upon the number of pages and the thickness of the paper you intend to use. Consult your printer.

Heavy, glossy cover stock, produces an attractive book. You may wish to use white or even color cover stock with black ink. When combined with xerography, it is relatively inexpensive for short runs. If you want to print colors other than black, you will have to find a color copier or have the covers printed offset.

Covers not only protect the text, they are an important sales tool. The front cover must be attractive (to encourage the customer to pick it up) and the back cover must contain your best sales copy (to encourage the customer to buy it). For a complete discussion of what should be included on the covers, see *Is There a Book Inside You?*, listed in the Appendix.

Some pasteup tips. A narrow strip of masking tape on the underside of your rules and triangles will prevent ink from flowing underneath during line scribing, which can create blobs and smudges. Mount the tape 1/16th" from the edge.

Rubber cement and thinner are easier to use on small jobs when kept in small plastic bottles with squirt tops.

Keep thinner off the face of strike-on (composer, typewriter, word processor) and laser type. The thinner may make the type discolor or run if the type is not thoroughly dry.

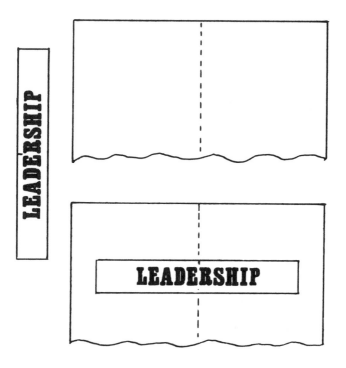

To center elements on the layout, measure and mark the center of the element with non-repro blue pen. This is most easily done with a center finding rule: one with the zero in the *middle*. Then mark the center line of the board and match up the two marks. This is much faster than measuring from the edges.

To divide an area into equal parts, place a ruler on an angle to any number on the ruler that is easily divisible by the number you wish to divide the area by. In the example, we want to make six equal columns so we angle the ruler to twelve. Mark off every two inches, remove the ruler and draw the vertical columns with the T square and triangle.

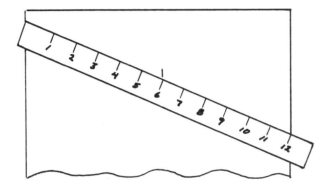

Stand back and visualize each pasted up page. Consider the advisability of adding dividers and borders to isolate certain areas or to make them stand out.

Trim elements as straight as possible to eliminate optical illusions. Irregularly cut blocks of type will appear to be out of line during pasteup.

Important charts, graphs and type should be positioned toward the outside of the book's pages (to the left on left-hand pages and to the right on right-hand pages) so they will not be swallowed by the binding in the "gutter."

Sharp pencils provide precise measuring. Measuring from marks made with a blunt pencil may lead to slanted lines and uneven columns. Keep pencils sharp by giving them a chisel edge on fine sandpaper.

Shadows may be seen by the camera if you paste on thick elements or if there are too many pieces of overlapping paper. Trim carefully and avoid thick layers.

Leave a one-eighth inch border when cutting out elements to be pasted down, whenever possible. They will be easier to handle and if you must do some opaquing to the edges, you are less liable to damage the type or artwork.

The rub-on sort of transfer type should be mounted on a separate piece of paper first and then transferred in one piece to the board. Do not work directly on the board. Formatt by Graphic Products Corporation is printed on a clear film which may be initially laid out on the edge of a rule prior to applying to the paper.

Use the same style of type throughout the book. Variations in type detract from the appearance. Select one size type for the text, another for captions, one for headlines, etc. Then, use them consistently.

Extensive rule and border work can be done much faster with preprinted transfer materials and rolls of black border tape. See your graphic arts shop.

When necessary, add space between paragraphs to make the first line flush with the top of the page and the last line flush with the bottom. When laying out two columns to a page, make the lines of type even so that they will rest on a rule placed straight across the page.

Don't cram too much onto a page. Most good layouts have a lot of "white space."

Keep it simple, this is the essence of good design. The most important consideration is the content of the book. Have confidence in your own sense of "what looks right." If the layout does not look right to you, it probably will not look right to your reader either.

This book covers only the basic mechanics of composition, layout and pasteup for short-run book production. For a comprehensive course in publishing your own book including all the elements of writing, book design, publishing, marketing and distribution, see *The Self-Publishing Manual*. This book tells you **how**, *The Self-Publishing Manual* will tell you **why**. See the listing in the Appendix.

Final proofing. It is always wise to give your book a final proofing for typos, content and layout. Do not proof the boards themselves since they could be damaged in the handling. Make photocopies of the boards and proof the copies by making your notations right on them. You may even send the copies off to someone else to proof; this is a good idea since they will notice things you have missed. Once the corrections are made, it is easy to check the marked-up photocopies against the boards to make sure none of the changes were overlooked.

Mailing. If you are mailing your work to be reproduced instead of dealing with a local print shop, here are a few tips. Rather than ship your only copy, make a photocopy for your files. In fact, it is a good idea to make photocopies periodically as you generate your manuscript. Store one copy away from your place of work to guard against losing it all in a fire or burglary.

Make sure the boards or negatives are complete, place them between two stiff pieces of cardboard and tape them together. Label the cardboard with your name and the name of the book. If there are photos, drawings or other materials which are not pasted down, package them separately in the same manner. The stiffened work may be slipped into a "Jiffy" type shipping bag, but a corrugated carton will protect them better.

Ship the work via United Parcel Service, overnight or two-day air. UPS insures all packages as part of the shipping price, and they get a signature on delivery. They rarely lose a package. If you must ship via the Postal Service, ship by air and insure. Under current Postal Regulations, manuscripts may be shipped via the cheaper "book rate" but this is not a time to be saving a few pennies.

Storage of originals. Cover each board with a slip sheet of plain paper and store the stack in a cool, dry, dark place.

For more information on pasteup and layout, see the books listed in the Appendix.

Chapter Five

Manufacture—Reproduction and Binding

This chapter is included not only to help you understand the processes involved but to explain to your copy shop and/or printer some of the new manufacturing techniques which are possible with their machines.

Techniques for manufacturing books in both short and long runs are explained. The methods you use will be selected depending upon the length of your print run and the machinery available.

Paper. Paper comes in various "basis weights"; the weighing systems used depend upon the grade of paper, so there will be some confusion in their nomenclature. For example, 20 lb. *bond* paper is close to 50 lb. *book* paper and cover stocks are often measured in point sizes (thickness).

Most xerographic machines will accept 16 to 32 lb. bond paper or the equivalent and the most common is the 20 lb. bond (Xerox #4042 dual-purpose paper). Book paper is more opaque (less see-through) than bond and is recommended for books since they are printed on both sides of the sheet. Both 60 lb. (Xerox 24 lb. #4024 d-pp) and 70 lb. (Xerox 28 lb. #4024 d-pp) book work well; the heavier paper should be used for shorter books, those under 100 pages, to provide more bulk. Before printing your book, make test copies on several different types of paper and check them for feel and opacity. If the book has just a few pages, make sure the paper is sufficiently heavy so it will bulk up for a good squared spine.

Book papers are available in white and off-white. International Paper Company describes their eggshell, antique, and others in their *Book Papers Sample Book*. Write 77 West 45th Street, New York, NY 10036.

Colors and special papers such as parchment are also available but all papers will not run well in xerographic and offset machines. Rely on your printer; let him or her supply the paper.

Cover stock. Xerographic machines such as the Xerox Model 9400 will handle cover stock up to about 12 pt. (.012 inches) but you will have to run tests as flexibility makes a difference too. Sometimes these machines will run as many as ten sheets, heat up and jam. Offset presses will usually handle much heavier stock. Common cover stocks are 10 pt. and 12 pt.

Book covers usually have a smooth, shiny surface on the outside. This material is called "C-1-S" or "Coated One Side."

Offset printed covers must be coated with a varnish or "press wax" or plastic coating so their ink will not rub off. But Xerography produces a hard non-smudge inking. Color cover stocks in the lighter shades are particularly nice when xerographed.

For white stock, see Ingram Paper's *King James Cover* in 12 pt., Zellerbach's 10 pt. and 12 pt. C-1-S Cover and BM&T's Kromekote Cover C-1-S in 10 pt. and 12 pt. For color cover stock, see Lindenmeyr Paper Corporation, 444-P North Michigan Avenue, Chicago, IL 60611. They have a large selection of regular and metallic colors in 10.5 pt.

The lighter cover stocks will produce a better binding as they flex more easily at the spine when the book is opened. If your print shop does not have cover stock, check the *Yellow Pages* under "paper" and get your own.

For color covers, the Xerox Model 6500 copier may be used in the short run, and regular offset printing may be used for larger quantities. The 6500 is very expensive but you should be aware of its existence. If you are printing just a few books and want color on the cover, it may be your answer. For the richest reproduction, run it on white cover stock and do not overlap the colors. The machine also does a nice job on color photographic slides. Experiment and consult your local printer. Other brands of color copiers are coming on the market. Check around.

If you have very nice full-color artwork and want just a few covers, here is a unique method of reproduction. Lay out the front cover, back cover and spine straight-across on a single board. Shoot it with a 35mm or 4 x 5 camera with color negative film. Instruct the photo lab to blow up the image in the color prints to precisely 5.5 x 8.5. Then install these prints as covers and trim as described later in this chapter. For added durability, you may wish to laminate or overspray the finished print.

Copiers. There are many different types of plain paper copiers. Some print both sides of the paper, some reduce the copy, some accept or produce odd sizes, some sort into bins and so on. For short-run book production the Xerox Models 9200 and 9400 are good while the 8200 and 9500 produce better copy. The 8200 and 9500 are the top of the line and do the best on solid areas and photographs up to 100 line. If the pasteups are on 20 lb. paper, the machines will feed them automatically (no hand feeding of individual sheets) and will run at the rate of 120 impressions per minute. The IBM Series III and some Kodak machines also reproduce both solids and photographs well. Print quality varies from machine to machine of the same type and adjustment makes a great difference. The best copies are often made right after a service call.

Coordinate your print run in advance with your copy shop. The end of the month is often their busiest time because that is when all the small community newsletters are being printed.

Offset duplicators. Offset duplicators are smaller printing presses and are common in the quick print shops. They take paper, plastic or metal plates and print on small sheets (not rolls) of paper. For example, the Multilith 1250, which has been around since 1935, will handle paper up to 10 x 15 while the Model 1250W will go to 11 x 17. The A.B. Dick 360 accepts paper to 11.75 x 17.

For short runs, the duplicator with metal plates is more expensive to operate than xerographic machines because of the required setup time. A photographic negative is "shot" from your pasted-up boards, the printing plate is "burned" from the negative and then the plate is placed on the press. Paper and plastic plates are cheaper and easier to use.

Photo direct offset. Photo direct offset is the system used by most of the high volume instant print centers. This newer technique skips the negative stage by photographically transferring the image directly from your pasted boards to the printing plate. The quality of the reproduction is just short of more expensive metal plates.

Commercial offset. This is a catch-all category which includes all of the larger regular commercial printers who use bigger offset presses with metal plates to produce high quality single to four (full) color work. If you plan a longer run for your book, you may wish to use one of these printers or even one who specializes in books.

See *The Self-Publishing Manual* for instructions on how to make up a "request for quotation" form. Send it to the thirty+ book printers listed. Only then will you know you are getting the best price.

Binding. Pamphlets may be *wire stitched* with side or spine positioned wire staples. The staples may be installed by hand, a booklet making machine or some photocopiers. The Xerox 1075 and 1090 copiers may be fitted with an Automatic Stapler Folder (ASF) attached which will fold and staple up to 15 sheets of 20 lb. stock plus a cover sheet of up to 90 lb. paper to create booklets of up to 64 pages.

Basically there are three types of book bindings and a few variations of each: mechanical (comb, spiral, Velo Bind), perfect (glued or softcover) and edition (casebound or hardcover). Book binding is an ancient hand-craft. See your library for the many books on the subject. Send to Bro Dart, 500 Arch Street, Williamsport, PA 17705 for a free copy of *Modern Simplified Book Repair.*

Mechanical binding consists of one of the many plastic or wire methods. Most produce a book which will open and lie flat. Most instant print shops have one or more of these machines. These binding systems are good for manuals and workbooks, but most will not produce a product which will pass for a bookstore-type book.

Perfect binding

Perfect (softcover) binding may be accomplished in any one of four ways. In order to print the title and author on the spine, a squared-off spine of 1/8th inch, minimum, is required; 1/4 inch (or more) is better.

1. The standard "perfect binding" technique uses a hot melt adhesive. This requires setup time, warm up time and sophisticated machinery. Some instant print shops may have a short-run machine such as the Bind-Fast from Standard Duplicating (Andover, MA 01810) or the Bind-O-Mat 200 while other shops will have to send the printed pages out to a bindery.

Normally it is not cost effective to set up a perfect binding machine for less than 500 books. Your job may have to wait until it can be "ganged" or consolidated with another one.

2. The Cheshire 750 binding machine may be used to install perfect-bound type covers as follows. Stack and bind the pages of the book in the machine with an 8.5" binding strip. Then score the cover twice so it will fold nicely around the pages and attach the cover with Scotch brand double stick cellophane tape. Match up the tape with the scoring on the

cover and carefully align the bound edge of the text. The machine will bind books up to 1.5." On very thick books, two strips of double stick tape may be required. This method produces a book which will open to lie flat and individual pages may even be added or removed later, if desired. To add or remove pages, wrap a clean piece of paper around the spine of the book to protect the printed title and insert it back into the machine set for "edit." Once the glue is warmed, simply pull out or add pages.

3. For very short runs and for making dummy books, use a cold, volatile adhesive such as Scotch brand contact cement. Brush the adhesive onto the edge of the text. A short, stiff brush will assure capture of all the pages. Score and fold the covers. Then reverse their folds to expose the channel to be glued. Brush the adhesive across this area. Avoid breathing the fumes or allowing the adhesive to come into contact with the skin. Allow the adhesive to set and then mate pages and cover carefully. Follow the directions on the bottle.

The process may be automated somewhat with a padding press. Stack the texts in the press, turn it so that the edges of the books point up, if possible, and brush the adhesive on the edges. After the adhesive sets, slit the books apart with a knife and install the sets into the covers. When using a padding press, first cover its edges with tape so that excess adhesive will not contact the edges of the press.

This contact cement method produces a much more flexible binding than a hot melt adhesive, allowing the book to open and lie perfectly flat. This system will even permit the use of larger fold-out pages for charts and maps.

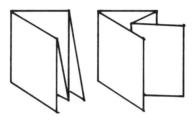

Examples of fold-out pages

For good perfect binding by hand, scoring of the covers is critical. Test various widths to assure a good fit. Many of the folding machines found in instant print shops have a scoring wheel. Often the covers must be sent through twice, once for each scoring. If a machine is not available, a rule and scoring tool or even a dull butter knife may be used. The trimming of softcover books is covered below.

4. Thermal binding machines may be used to install soft covers on books though there are some limitations. These machines use manufacturer-supplied 8.5 x 11 report covers with an adhesive strip in the spine. The machines heat and melt the adhesive and force the pages of the report into the glue. These covers may be printed but they cannot be passed through xerographic copiers because the heat will melt the adhesive. Once installed, the covers must be cut down to 5.5 x 8.5 book size. Some of the manufacturers of thermal binding machines are General Binding Corporation, One GBC Plaza,

Northbrook, IL 60062; Mitey-Bind, 10 Paterson Avenue, Newton, NJ 07860; Swingline, 32-00 Skillman Avenue, Long Island City, NY 11101, the Bindit available from Heyden, 7 East Winnwood Drive, Winnwood, PA and Cheshire.

Edition, case or hardcover bindings may be installed in short runs in any of five ways.

1. Hand binding. This is the original way. Get a book on binding from your library. For a hand binding kit with complete instructions, get *Publish Your Own Handbound Books* by Betty Doty from The Bookery, 8193-P Riata, Redding, CA 96002.

2. Local book bindery. These hand binding shops are fast disappearing as their craftsmen are passing away but you may have one in your community. The cost may be $5 to $10 per book; such an expensive price may be acceptable if you want only a few copies for presentation. Contact the bindery before the book is printed to ask how they want the printed sheets. For a list of book binders in your area, contact the Library Binding Institute, 150 Allens Creek Road, Rochester, NY 14618-3308.

3. Rebinding companies will hardcover your pages for about $6.50 each (10 minimum), less for larger quantities. Check for local companies in the *Yellow Pages* and compare their prices with the book binders listed in the Appendix.

4. Cheshire offers hard covers in 3/8," 3/4" and 1" spines to accept pages bound in their binding machine. These covers are very easy to install but

are only available in a 8.5 x 11 size. They cost about $2 each and come in red, blue and brown. See your local Xerox Corporation office.

5. Velo Bind provides some of the most attractive and certainly the strongest of the hard cover bindings. There are a variety of colors and a simple machine makes installation easy. Though standard sizes are 8.5 x 11, 13 and 14, a smaller size (A-5) suitable for 5.5 x 8.5 books is available on special order. Spine sizes are 1/4" to 3" in nine increments. For details on covers and equipment, write Velo Bind, Inc. at 650-P Almanor Avenue, Sunnyvale, CA 94086.

Trimming. After softcover books are bound, they must be trimmed to make their edges even. Placed in a large guillotine-like trimmer, just a fraction of an inch is sliced off the top, side and bottom. Books may be stacked several deep and trimmed in a single slice. This results in a book which measures slightly less than, for example, 5.5 x 8.5. Most medium-sized instant print shops will have a trimmer.

For very short runs, be careful in binding to even up the top and bottom of the sheets. Then only the wrap-around cover will have to be trimmed.

If a trimmer is not available, a few books may be cut by hand. Draw a light line on the inside of the cover using the pages as a straightedge. Then open the book, place a metal straightedge on the line and cut along it with a razor knife. The result will be very professional.

Stamping. Covers may be marked with foil stamping or silk screening. Many instant printers have these machines for applying the title and name of the author to the outside of the hardcover book.

Stampers are available from The Kwik Print Manufacturing Co., 4868-P Victor Street, Jacksonville, FL 32207; General Binding Corporation, One GBC Plaza, Northbrook, IL 60062 and Kingsley Machine, 850-P Cahuenga Blvd., Hollywood, CA 90038.

Storage of unbound pages. Store any unbound pages flat, out of the sun, in a cool, dry place. Heat and humidity make the photocopier toner sticky while sunlight will yellow the paper.

Afterword

People have been manufacturing their own books for centuries. Now it is your turn to carry on the tradition and discover the rewards and satisfaction of book publishing.

Once you have finished this book, you are ready for *Is There a Book Inside You?* and *The Self-Publishing Manual*. Visit the shop where you found this book or use the order blank on the last page.

Contact me at Para Publishing for a free book publishing information kit. We will also place you on the mailing list for our free publishing newsletter.

Once you do publish, please send a copy of your new book for my shelf—autographed of course.

s/ Dan Poynter

Appendix

Resources - for more information

Books and Reports

These are specially selected books on various aspects of researching, writing, typesetting, printing, promoting, marketing and distributing books. I have not listed every book on these subjects, what you find here is a selection of the best. I use them daily in my work and highly recommend them to you. As a service, they may be ordered from Para Publishing. See the order blank.

Writing and Editing

Is There a Book Inside You? How to Successfully Author a Book Alone or Through Collaboration by Dan Poynter and Mindy Bingham. Now you can *author* a book whether or not you have the time to become a good *writer*. Books are rarely the effort of only one person. In today's high-demand world, thousands of authors, without the time or ability to write, are relying on experienced professionals to do the editing, co-authoring, or even ghost writing. This book reveals how to find, interview, negotiate, contract and work with writing partners such as editors, researchers, contract workers, co-authors, and ghost writers. *Is There a Book Inside You?* will show you how to pick your topic, how to break the project down into easy-to-attack pieces, how and where to do research: improve your material, a step-by-step process that makes writing (almost) easy, and more. A Writer's Digest Book Club main selection.

ISBN 0-915516-42-X Softcover, 5.5 x 8.5 240 pages $9.95

Writing with Precision by Jefferson D. Bates. A practical and systematic approach to writing clearly and precisely. A good resource with numerous examples and fun to read. Should be read by every author before writing a manuscript and every publisher before editing a book.

ISBN 0-87491-185-0 Softcover, 6 x 9 226 pages $7.95

Write Right! by Jan Venolia. This desk drawer digest of punctuation, grammar and style is an important reference which should be next to your dictionary. Demonstrating proper usage with quotes from literature and politics, *Write Right!* makes editing manuscripts easy and fun. This style manual is essential when copy editing.

ISBN 0-89815-061-2 Softcover, 5.5 x 7 127 pages $4.95

Copyright Not Copycat by Sally Stuart and Woody Young explains the new copyright law. The authors show you how much research material you may legally use and how to protect your work from others. They cover fair use, permissions, licensing, foreign protection, registration procedures and much more. Examples of forms. Glossary.

ISBN 0-939513-51-X Softcover, 8.5 x 11 98 pages $9.95

Pasteup and Layout

Complete Guide to Pasteup by Walter B. Graham is a definitive course in preparing camera-ready copy for printing. Graham reveals numerous time-saving and money-saving pasteup secrets and shortcuts. Clear step-by-step procedures for books and brochures; generously illustrated. If you perform pasteup functions or supervise pasteup, you need this book. Illustrated glossary. One of our top sellers.

ISBN 0-912920-40-8 Softcover, 8.5 x 11 216 pages $19.95

Desktop Publishing and Typesetting by Michael Kleper is a goldmine of book production information. Whether you are looking into laser typesetting for the first time or are a power computer user, this book will be a constant reference. An exhaustive 770 pages.

ISBN 0-8306-0700-5 Softcover, 8.5 x 11 770 pages $29.95

Printing

Pocket Pal, A Graphic Arts Production Handbook from International Paper. This is the best basic reference on pre-press and printing. It provides specifications and descriptions for paper (weight, comparisons, etc.), inks, copy preparation, film imposition, the mechanics of printing, binding and much, much more. Invaluable reference; you will always look it up in *Pocket Pal* first.

Order #91838 Softcover, 4.25 x 7.5 216 pages $6.95

Getting it Printed, How to work with Printers and Graphic Arts Services to Assure Quality, Stay on Schedule and Control Costs by Mark Beach, Steve Shepro and Ken Russon. An extraordinary text for anyone who plans, designs or buys printing. Avoid costly mistakes by learning the processes as well as how to buy typesetting, layout services and printing effectively. Good glossary, resources. You will treasure this beautiful book.

ISBN 0-9602664-7-X Softcover, 8.5 x 11 236 pages $29.95

Buying Book Printing answers the question we hear most: How to find the best and least expensive printer for your particular book. Each printer is set up to manufacture certain kinds of books. Specialties vary depending on type of binding, book measurements, print-run, etc. This report shows you how to make up a *Request for Quotation* and provides a mailing list of printers who specialize in book manufacture. A section on **color** printing describes how to contact local representatives of Hong Kong and other foreign printers. This report will save you thousands of dollars in printing, binding and trucking costs. Includes forms and resources.

ISBN 0-915516-55-1 8.5 x 11 report 35 pages $14.95

Publishing

The Self-Publishing Manual, How to write, Print, and Sell Your Own Book by Dan Poynter is a concentrated short course in writing, publishing, marketing, promoting and distributing books. Now in its fourth revised edition, this is the book writers, printers and publishers say "I wish I had a year ago." It takes the reader step-by-step from idea, through manuscript, printing, promotion, and sales. Along with an in-depth study of the publishing industry, the book explains in detail numerous innovative book marketing techniques. The Manual is the *Bible* for writers and a constant reference for publishers. Absolutely the best book on publishing, promotion and distribution.

ISBN 0-915516-37-3 Softcover, 5.5 x 8.5 352 pages $14.95

Publishing Forms, A Collection of Applications and Information for the Beginning Publisher by Dan Poynter. With this kit, a new book can be listed in all directories easily, submitted to all wholesalers properly, and registered with all agencies correctly. Assembled into a 9 x 12 folder, there are over 200 pages of forms and instructions such as applications for ABI, LC, copyright and many directory listings. Where appropriate, these are the actual multi-part forms, not reprints. New book approval forms make wholesaler contact easy. As a bonus, all the important reviewers and wholesaler addresses are supplied on pressure-sensitive labels, ready to use.

ISBN 0-915516-38-1 Folder, 9 x 12 Over 200 pages $14.95

In Cold Type by Leonard Shatzkin provides the most detailed and thorough inside account of book publishing. He shows why it is so easy for the smaller and newer publisher to successfully compete with the big established New York houses. **Warning**: this book is slow reading because you will highlight every other sentence. Must reading.

ISBN 0-395-34643-6 Softcover, 5.5 x 8.5 397 pages $8.95

How to Get Happily Published by Judith Appelbaum and Nancy Evans. How to write, find a publisher, locate an agent or publish yourself by two women with years of varied experience in New York publishing. Learn how book publishing works. This is a gold mine of publishing information with a lengthy resource section.

ISBN 0-452-25332-2 Softcover, 5.25 x 8 271 pages $6.95

Book Fairs, An Exhibiting Guide for Publishers, by Dan Poynter contains everything you need to select, arrange and operate a booth at a book fair. Required reading for first time exhibitors and a helpful reminder/checklist for the seasoned veteran. So good, parts were extracted for reprint in *Publishers Weekly*.

ISBN 0-915516-43-8 Softcover, 5.5 x 8.5 96 pages $7.95

Promotion

How to Get Publicity and Make the Most of it Once You've Got it by William Parkhurst. Get your name in the papers, your voice on the radio, your face on TV. How to book and conduct radio, television and print interviews. Parkhurst covers writing news releases, designing press kits and more. Good, solid and practical with an insider's expertise. Like having your own publicist on your bookshelf. No author wants to be surprised in an interview situation. Excellent reference.

ISBN 0-8129-1161-X Hardcover, 6 x 8.5 245 pages $14.95

Publicity for Books and Authors by Peggy Glenn shows authors and publishers how to get free and effective publicity for their books. The author shares her own experiences on television talk shows, radio, with magazines and newspapers— what worked and what did not. Author/publisher Glenn knows the theory of promotion, practices it with success and teaches it well. Examples and ideas.

ISBN 0-936930-91-8 Softcover, 8.5 x 11 182 pages $12.95

Copy Writer's Handbook, A Practical Guide for Advertising and Promotion of Specialized and Scholarly Books and Journals by Nat G. Bodian. How to draft copy for space ads, direct mail promotions, book covers; copy fitting, headline writing, using reviews, testimonials and more. Many book promotion case histories illustrate this excellent reference. Don't draft advertising copy without this book.

ISBN 0-89495-039-8 Softcover, 6.75 x 10.5 277 Pages $19.95

Marketing

Successful Direct Marketing Methods by Bob Stone. This is the *Bible* for marketing your book via direct mail, magazines, newspapers and broadcasting direct to your reader. "Direct Marketing" is where smaller publishers of narrow-market books have the advantage over the big New York publishers. Learn how to select lists and media to go direct to your customers at the least possible cost. A well-known book by a master in the field. Highly recommended. Glossary.

ISBN 0-87251-040-9 Hardcover, 7.5 x 9.5 370 pages $29.95

Guerrilla Marketing, Secrets for Making Big Profits From Your Small Business by Jay Conrad Levinson. How to get the most out of brochures, telephone marketing, classified ads, the *Yellow Pages*, newspapers, radio, TV, direct mail, seminars and much, much more. *Guerrilla Marketing* is a game plan to cut your costs, increase your profits and give you the winning edge. Full of valuable, creative ideas.

ISBN 0-395-38314-5 Softcover, 6 x 9 226 pages $8.95

Book Marketing: A New Approach by Dan Poynter is a low-cost marketing plan for your book. It leads you through the three-step plan for selling direct to the buyer, the five-step plan for selling to bookstores, the seven-step plan for libraries, all the subsidiary rights and our specialty: the more lucrative non-traditional markets. **Start with this report.**

ISBN 0-915516-58-6 8.5 x 11 Report 64 pages $14.95

101 Ways to Market Your Books by John Kremer is simply a most creative, informational and useful manual on book publishing. Kremer writes from detailed research and hard-earned experience. He covers advertising, promotion, distributors, bookstores, book design, libraries, spinoffs, and much more. In fact, there is little he does not cover and cover well.

ISBN 0-912411-09-0 Softcover, 6 x 9 304 pages $14.95

The Publisher's Direct Mail Handbook by Nat Bodian. This is the very last word on direct mail marketing as it applies to books. Full of facts and figures, it is easy and fun to read. Bodian summarizes all the other books on direct mail advertising. Read Stone first and then this book to *earn your degree* in book marketing. Highly recommended.

ISBN 0-89495-079-7 Hardcover, 7 x 10.5 256 pages $39.95

Book Reviews by Dan Poynter shows you in detail how to take advantage of the free publicity available to books from the pre-publication galleys to a continuing review program. Book reviews are the least expensive and most effective form of book promotion. Reviews are not hard to get if you follow the unwritten (until now) rules. This report provides paint-by-the-numbers instructions for making galleys and describes in a detailed action plan how to set up a review program so your books will be reviewed again and again. Examples and resources.

ISBN 0-915516-56-X 8.5 x 11 Report 45 pages $24.95

News Releases and Book Publicity shows you how to draft news releases and other publicity for your books. After book reviews, news releases are your most effective and least expensive form of book promotion. Yet, few publishers use or even know about news releases. If you are not sending out a news release every 30 days, get this report. Step-by-step instructions, paint-by-the-numbers format outlines, many examples and resources are included.

ISBN 0-915516-52-7 8.5 x 11 Report 46 pages $19.95

Direct Mail for Book Publishers shows how you can compete with the larger publishers by taking your message direct to the reader. Study the rules of direct mail such as repetition, timing, response formulas and profit analysis. Learn to find and evaluate lists. Follow the plan for drafting your brochure and cover letter; assemble a direct mail package that brings results.

ISBN 0-915516-59-4 8.5 x 11 Report 54 pages $19.95

Publishing Law and Contracts

Author Law & Strategies by Brad Bunnin and Peter Beren is a complete legal guide for the working writer. The authors provide easy-to-understand practical advice on contracts, copyright, defamation, collaboration, and agent agreements. This essential reference answers the questions and provides examples. Sample contracts.

ISBN 0-917316-59-2 Softcover, 8.5 x 11 296 pages $14.95

Publishing Agreements by Charles Clark contains the vital information most publishers request from us: samples of publishing contracts. Actual contracts are reproduced with each paragraph explained on the facing page. Some of the contracts are: general author-publisher, educational author-publisher, paperback rights, translator's agreement, merchandise rights agreement, sound reproductions rights, etc. Even more valuable if you are considering foreign rights sales or if you sign authors. Imported from Great Britain.

ISBN 0-04-655015-1 Hardcover, 5.5 x 9 185 pages $19.50

Magazines for Authors and Publishers

Write for a sample copy and current subscription rates.

American Bookseller (Bookstore news)
122 East 42nd Street
New York, NY 10168

American Libraries (Library news)
50 East Huron Street
Chicago, IL 60611

Canadian Author & Bookman
P.O. Box 120
Niagara-On-The-Lake, ON
Canada L0S 1J0

The College Store Journal
528 East Lorain Street
Oberlin, OH 44074

The Horn Book Magazine (Children's books)
Park Square Building
31 St. James Street
Boston, MA 02116

Info World
1060 Marsh Road #C-200
Menlo Park, CA 94025

Library Journal
249 West 17th Street
New York, NY 10011

Miniature Book News
16 Dromara Road
St. Louis, MO 63124

Publishers Weekly
249 West 17th Street
New York, NY 10011

Personal Publishing
P.O. Box 390
Itaska, IL 60143

Publish!
555 De Haro Street
San Francisco, CA 94107

School Library Journal
249 West 17th Street
New York, NY 10011

Small Press Magazine
11-P Ferry Lane West
Westport, CT 06880

Small Press Review
P.O. Box 100-P
Paradise, CA 95969

Step-By-Step Graphics
P.O. Box 1901-P
Peoria, IL 61656-9979

Typeworld
15 Oakridge Circle
Wilmington, MA 01887

The Writer
8 Arlington Street
Boston, MA 02116

Writer's Digest
1507 Dana Avenue
Cincinnati, OH 45207

Newsletters for Authors and Publishers

Write for a sample copy and current subscription rates.

Author's Newsletter
P.O. Box 32008-P
Phoenix, AZ 85064

Computer Aided Publishing Report
InfoVision, Inc.
52 Dragon Court
Woburn, MA 01801

Editorial Eye
85 South Bragg Street
Alexandria, VA 22312-2731

The Huenefeld Report
P.O. Box UP
Bedford, MA 01730

IBM Composer Network
Berkeley Publishing
1701-AP Grove
Berkeley, CA 94709

MicroPublishing Report
21150 Hawthorne Blvd #104-P
Torrance, CA 90503

Publishing Poynters
P.O. Box 4232-446
Santa Barbara, CA 93140-4232

Towers Club USA Newsletter
P.O. Box 2038-P
Vancouver, WA 98668

Professional Organizations

Write for an application and inquire about benefits and dues. Many associations publish a magazine or newsletter.

Publishers Marketing Association
P.O. Box 299-P
Hermosa Beach, CA 90254

Association of Canadian Publishers
70 The Esplanade, Third Floor
Toronto, ON M5E 1R2

The Authors Guild
234 West 44th Street
New York, NY 10036

COSMEP (Committee Of Small Magazine Editors and Publishers)
P.O. Box 703-P
San Francisco, CA 94101

Independent Publishers Guild
52 Chepstow Road
London W2
Great Britain

Marin Self-Publishers Association
P.O. Box 343-P
Ross, CA 94957

National Writers Club
1450 South Havana #620-P
Aurora, CO 80012

Graphic Arts and Printing Supplies

Send for current catalog.

A.H. Gaebel, Inc.
P.O. Box 5-P
East Syracuse, NY 13057

Artmaster (Clip art)
550-P North Claremont Blvd.
Claremont, CA 91711

Basic Crafts Co. (Bookbinding supplies)
1201-P Broadway
New York, NY 10001

Caddylak Systems (Clip art: borders, etc.)
201-P Montrose Road
Westbury, NY 11590

Creative Media (Clip art)
P.O. Box 5955-P
Berkeley, CA 94705

Dot Pasteup Supplies (Catalog)
1612-P California Street
Omaha, NE 68102

Draphix
3865-P Elm Street
Denver, CO 80207

Dynamic Graphics (Clip art)
P.O. Box 1901-P
Peoria, IL 61656-1901

Graphics Master (Graphics catalog)
P.O. Box 46086-P
Los Angeles, CA 90046

Hartco Products (Catalog)
226-P West Pearl Street
West Jefferson, OH 43162

Midwest Publishers Supply (Catalog)
4640 North Olcott Avenue
Chicago, IL 60656

Norman H. Ludlow (Clip art)
516-P Arnett Blvd.
Rochester, NY 14619

The Printers Shopper (Catalog)
111-P Press Lane
Chula Vista, CA 92010

Volk Corp. (Clip Art)
1401-P North Main Street
Pleasantville, NJ 08232

Book Binders

These companies can install hard cover (case binding) on your pages. Write for brochures.

Sam Har Press,
Story House Corp.
Charlotteville, NY 12036.

Admundsen Publishing Co.
108 Washington Street
Decorah, IA 52101

Grimm Book Bindery
6880 Gisholt Road
Madison, WI 53713

American Econo-Clad
P.O. Box 1777-P
Topeka, KS 66601

Courses, Conferences and Seminars

Write for schedules and prices.

Walter B. Graham Pasteup Seminars
P.O. Box 369-P
Omaha, NE 68101 USA

Poynter's Book Publishing Seminars
P.O. Box 4232-446
Santa Barbara, CA 93140-4232
(805) 968-7277

Huenefeld Publishing Seminars
P.O. Box UP
Bedford, MA 01730

Glossary

Here are brief definitions of the more important word processing, pasteup, copying and printing terms.

BASIS WEIGHT: The weight of a ream of 500 sheets of paper based on a standard size for each type of paper. The sizes vary for book, bond, index, etc. One ream of 80 lb. bond will weigh 80 lbs.

BENDAY: Various density screens printed on an adhesive-backed plastic sheet which may be pasted to artwork. The screening provides tonal qualities to artwork.

BINDING: The processes following printing: folding, gathering, stitching, gluing, trimming and/or casing a book.

BLUE LINE: A proof sheet made by exposing a negative to a photosensitive paper. A blue print.

BODY TYPE: The majority of the type used in a book. Not a headline.

BOLDFACE: Type which is **heavier** than the text type with which it is used.

BOND: A hard finish rag or sulphite paper used for stationery and forms.

BOOKLET: A small book, usually with less than 48 pages.

BORDER: A frame around type or artwork.

CAMERA-READY: A completely prepared pasteup which is ready for the camera or xerographic reproduction. No further graphic arts work is required.

CASE BOUND: Hardcover or edition binding.

CHARACTER: a letter, number, punctuation mark or space in printed matter.

CLIP ART: Line drawings, screened pictures and illustrations designed to be cut out and pasted up.

COATED PAPER: Paper manufactured with a variety of surfaces which may be smooth, glossy or matte.

COLD TYPE: Strike-on type, such as that produced by a typewriter or IBM Composer, or photocomposition type. Not hot metal type.

COLLATING: Gathering of printed sheets into proper order for binding.

COMPOSITION: Typeset material. Typeset text ready to be pasted up.

CONTRAST: The degree of difference between the lightest and darkest parts of a picture.

CROP MARKS: The lines used to define the desired limits of the area of a photograph or illustration to be reproduced.

DENSITY: The relative darkness of an image area. In photography, the blackening or light stopping ability of a photographic image as numerically measured by a densiometer.

DISPLAY TYPE: Type which is larger than the text as in a chapter headline.

DUMMY: A preliminary mock-up of a book folded to the exact size of the finished job.

DUMMY FOLIO: "Working" page numbers added for identification purposes but changed before the book is printed.

EDIT: Changing, correcting or altering typed text into the required form.

FLAT: A printing term describing the assembling of negatives on a heavy paper sheet for platemaking. See stripping.

FLOPPY DISK: A flexible magnetic disc which stores data in a word processor or computer.

FOLIO: Page number.

GANG RUN (GANGING): Putting numerous unrelated jobs together for printing by assembling them on a single printing plate. Provides lower costs by economizing on setup charges.

GRIPPER MARGIN: The unprintable edge of the sheet of paper where the printing press or photocopier clamps the sheet to pull it through the printing machine. Often on top of the sheet and usually .25".

GUTTER: The space between columns of type such as the inner margins in two facing pages of a book.

HAIRLINE: A very finely ruled line.

HALFTONE: A screened photograph. A tone pattern composed of dots of uniform density but varying in size. A reproduction of a photograph whereby the various tones (highlights and shadows) are translated into numerous tiny dots for printing.

HALFTONE SCREEN: A screen placed in front of the negative material in the process camera to break up a continuous tone image into dots of black and white to produce a halftone. There are two types: ruled glass screens and contact screens.

HIGHLIGHTS: The lightest (or whitest) portions of a photograph or art work.

JUSTIFICATION: Composing lines of running text so that the left and right margins are even. Automatically performed by computerized typesetting machines.

LAYOUT: A sketch or preliminary drawing of what is to be printed. A mockup.

LEADING: The amount of vertical spacing, measured in points, between lines of typeset text. Rhymes with "heading."

LEAFLET: A printed piece of paper folded in the center to produce four pages.

LINE SHOT: Any negative, print, copy or printing plate which is composed of solid image areas without halftone patterns.

LINE DRAWING: A black and white drawing with no gray tones. Line art.

MANUSCRIPT: The book (typed or handwritten) before it is typeset, pasted up and printed.

MARGIN: The white space around the copy on a page.

MATTE: A non-shiny, dull surface.

MECHANICAL: See Pasteup.

MICROPROCESSOR: An electronic device capable of processing information in accordance with predefined instructions. The heart of a computer.

NEGATIVE: The image obtained from the original in the conventional photographic process. The tones are the reverse of those in the original subject. Positive prints are made from negatives.

NON-PHOTO BLUE: A light blue pencil or ink which will not be picked up by a plate making camera. Light blue pens and pencils are used to mark pasted up sheets.

OCR: Optical Character Recognition. A device that can recognize (read) typewritten characters and convert them to electronic impulses for translation to output media language. An OCR reader can read a printed page into a computer for editing and (revised) printout.

OFFSET LITHOGRAPHY: Where the image is transferred from the printing plate to a rubber blanket and then to, or "offset" on, the paper. Practically all lithography is done by the offset method.

PASTEUP: An array of reproduction quality copy arranged in proper position on a paper prepared as line copy ready for the camera. Same as a mechanical.

PERFECT BINDING: The standard glued-on cover seen on most softcovered books. It has a squared-off spine on which the title and name of the author may be printed. Also called "cold type."

PHOTOCOMPOSITION: Setting type photographically by exposing a photosensitive paper or film to images of typed characters in such a sequence as to create the desired text or copy.

PHOTODIRECT: Exposing an image directly to a light sensitive offset plate material.

PHOTOMECHANICAL TRANSFER, PMT, DIFFUSION TRANSFER: A photographic method in which the pasteup is exposed to a sheet of sensitized paper, the paper is processed in contact with a receiver sheet and the sheets are peeled apart to produce a usable image on the receiver.

PHOTOSTAT (OR STAT): A photographic reproduction—which can be negative or positive—made from film, artwork, other stats, etc., and used as line art for many art applications.

PLATE, PRINTING: Usually the master device bearing the image to be printed. May be paper, plastic or metal.

PLUGGING: A press condition whereby photographs appear muddy or characters fill in. Caused by poor plate burning, over application of ink or incorrect ink/water balance.

POSITIVE: A photographic image in which the tones correspond to the original subject. A positive on paper is usually called a "print."

QUICK PRINTING: Producing a printing plate or master directly from the original boards (pasteups) to reproduce multiple copies.

REVERSE: To print an image white on black, rather than black on white.

SADDLE STITCH: See stitch.

SCORING: Creasing or pressing a line into paper so that it will fold more readily and more accurately.

SCREEN: See halftone screen.

SHEET: Two printed pages, one on each side of a leaf of paper. If the sheet is folded to create four printed pages, it is called a "leaflet."

SIGNATURE: A part of a book obtained by folding a large single sheet of paper into sections. A book signature may contain 8, 16, 32, or 64 pages.

STITCH: A staple. The staple seen in magazines and brochures are "saddle stitches."

STRIKE-ON TYPE: Cold type created with a typewriter, Composer or computer character printer where the typeface makes an impression on paper through a (carbon) ribbon.

STRIPPING: The assembling of photographic negatives or positives and attaching them to the flat (a large sheet of heavy paper) for plate making.

TEXT: The main body of the page. Not the headlines.

TRANSFER TYPE: Sheets of characters, numerals, borders or symbols which may be burnished onto paper and added to the pasteup.

TRIM MARKS: Lines made on the edges of a camera-ready board to indicate where the page will be cut (trimmed) after it is printed.

TRIM SIZE: The size of the page once trimmed to its final dimension.

VELOX: A positive print of a photograph or line art ready for pasteup. Usually 65-, 85- or 100-line screen is used for photographs to produce "halftones."

WAX: An adhesive material used like rubber cement to attach elements to the pasteup board.

WHITE-OUT: Removing unwanted parts of a pasteup by covering with an opaque liquid.

WINDOW: A sheet of red, orange or black paper or acetate on a pasteup to indicate where a photograph will be positioned. These colors photograph as black creating a clear "window" in the black negative.

Colophon

This book is an example of the production system it describes. The first print run was xerographed while the larger second, third, fourth, and fifth runs were printed offset.

The techniques for joining all the existing typesetting, printing and binding processes, as is or modified, were developed by the author. Total production time for the first edition, excluding the development of the processes and drafting the text, took less than two days.

The first printing: March 1980
Typesetting: Xerox Model 850 word processor.
Layout and pasteup: Most pages were done on the 850.
Printing: Xerox Model 9400 copier at Kinko's Graphics by Cole, Goleta, California. Time: six minutes.
Binding: by hand with contact cement as described herein.
Trimming: by hand as described herein.
Print run: ten copies (a test).
Paper: Springhill 70 lb. book.

The second (revised) printing: May 1980
The revisions and typesetting were done on the 850.
Printing: Offset with metal plates at Kinko's Graphics by Cole, Goleta, California.
Binding: Perfect bound by Mackintosh & Young, Santa Barbara, California.
Print run: 3,000 copies.
Paper: Springhill 70 lb. book.

The third (revised) printing: December 1981
The revisions and typesetting were done on a Xerox 860 word processor.
Printing and Binding: Offset with standard book production techniques by Delta Lithograph, Van Nuys, California.
Print run: 5,000 copies.
Paper: 60 lb. offset vellum, cover 10 pt. C1S.
Cover art: Fraser Graphics.

The fourth (revised) printing: February 1987
The revisions were made on an "IBM compatible" Compaq 286 with Microsoft *Word* with the *Word Finder* thesaurus and SoftCraft's *Laser Fonts.*

The type was set on a Hewlett-Packard LaserJet Plus in the *Classic* typeface on Xerox 4024 copier paper.

Printing and Binding: Offset with standard book production techniques by Delta Lithograph, Valencia, California.

Print run: 5,000 copies
Paper: 60 lb. white offset book
Cover: 12 pt. C1S with UV plastic coat
Cover art: Robert Howard Graphic Design

The fifth (revised) printing: August 1988
The revisions were made on an "IBM compatible" Compaq 386 with Microsoft *Word* and *Ventura Publisher*. Type was set on an Apple LaserWriter II NT with New Century Schoolbook Typeface on Xerox 4024 copier paper.

Printing and binding by McNaughton & Gunn, Ann Arbor, Michigan.

Print run: 5,000 copies.
Paper: 60 lb. white offset book
Cover: 12 pt C1S with plastic laminate.
Cover art: Robert Howard Graphic Design

Index

(　) How to Get Happily Published @ $6.95
(　) How to Get Publicity @ $14.95
(　) In Cold Type @ $8.95
(　) Is There a Book Inside You? @ $9.95
(　) News Releases @ $19.95
(　) Pocket Pal @ $6.95
(　) Publicity for Books & Authors @ $12.95
(　) Publisher's Direct Mail Handbook @ $39.95
(　) Publishing Agreements @ $19.50
(　) Publishing Forms @ $14.95
(　) Successful Direct Marketing Methods @ $29.95
(　) The Self-Publishing Manual @ $14.95
(　) Write Right! @ $4.95
(　) Writing with Precision @ $7.95

Ship to:
Company name:_____

Your name_____

Address:_____

City: _____ State:____ZIP_____-_____

Daytime Telephone: (　) _____

Signature: _____

Payment:
(　) Here is my check
Please charge my (　) Visa, (　) AMEX or (　) MasterCard

Card number: _____ Exp. date: ____/____

Shipping:
(　) Book rate: $1.75 for the first book and .75 for each additional book (surface shipping may take three to four weeks in the U.S.; up to four months foreign.)
(　) Air Mail: $3 per book.

Sales tax:
Add 6% sales tax for shipments to California addresses.

Order Blank

To: **Para Publishing**
Dan Poynter
P.O. Box 4232-446
Santa Barbara, CA 93140-4232 USA

Telephone orders:
Call toll free 1(800) PARAPUB. Have your Visa AMEX or MasterCard ready.

Fax orders:
Fill out this form and fax to (805) 968-1379

Postal orders:
( ) I am enclosing $ _____. Please send the following books and reports. I understand I may return any of them for a full refund—for any reason, no questions asked.

( ) I do not wish to order now but please **add me to your mailing list** so I will receive future offers and publishing information.

( ) 101 Ways to Market Your Books @ $14.95
( ) Author Law & Strategies @ $14.95
( ) Book Fairs @ $7.95
( ) Book Marketing: A New Approach @ $14.95
( ) Book Reviews @ $24.95
( ) Buying Book Printing @ $14.95
( ) Complete Guide to Pasteup @ $19.95
( ) Copyright not Copycat @ $9.95
( ) Copy Writer's Handbook @ $19.95
( ) Desktop Publishing & Typesetting @ $29.95
( ) Direct Mail for Book Publishers @ $19.95
( ) Getting it Printed @ $29.95
( ) Guerrilla Marketing @ $8.95

Please turn over